FIXED INCOME ANALYSIS WORKBOOK

CFA Institute is the premier association for investment professionals around the world, with over 124,000 members in 145 countries. Since 1963 the organization has developed and administered the renowned Chartered Financial Analyst® Program. With a rich history of leading the investment profession, CFA Institute has set the highest standards in ethics, education, and professional excellence within the global investment community, and is the foremost authority on investment profession conduct and practice. Each book in the CFA Institute Investment Series is geared toward industry practitioners along with graduate-level finance students and covers the most important topics in the industry. The authors of these cutting-edge books are themselves industry professionals and academics and bring their wealth of knowledge and expertise to this series.

FIXED INCOME ANALYSIS WORKBOOK

Third Edition

Barbara S. Petitt, CFA

Jerald E. Pinto, CFA

Wendy L. Pirie, CFA

with

Robin Grieves, CFA
Gregory M. Noronha, CFA

WILEY

Cover image: © iStock.com / PPAMPicture
Cover design: Wiley

Copyright © 2015 by CFA Institute. All rights reserved.

Published by John Wiley & Sons, Inc., Hoboken, New Jersey.
The First and Second Editions were published by Wiley in 2000 and 2007.
Published simultaneously in Canada.

No part of this publication may be reproduced, stored in a retrieval system, or transmitted in any form or by any means, electronic, mechanical, photocopying, recording, scanning, or otherwise, except as permitted under Section 107 or 108 of the 1976 United States Copyright Act, without either the prior written permission of the Publisher, or authorization through payment of the appropriate per-copy fee to the Copyright Clearance Center, Inc., 222 Rosewood Drive, Danvers, MA 01923, (978) 750-8400, fax (978) 646-8600, or on the Web at www.copyright.com. Requests to the Publisher for permission should be addressed to the Permissions Department, John Wiley & Sons, Inc., 111 River Street, Hoboken, NJ 07030, (201) 748-6011, fax (201) 748-6008, or online at www.wiley.com/go/permissions.

Limit of Liability/Disclaimer of Warranty: While the publisher and author have used their best efforts in preparing this book, they make no representations or warranties with respect to the accuracy or completeness of the contents of this book and specifically disclaim any implied warranties of merchantability or fitness for a particular purpose. No warranty may be created or extended by sales representatives or written sales materials. The advice and strategies contained herein may not be suitable for your situation. You should consult with a professional where appropriate. Neither the publisher nor author shall be liable for any loss of profit or any other commercial damages, including but not limited to special, incidental, consequential, or other damages.

For general information on our other products and services or for technical support, please contact our Customer Care Department within the United States at (800) 762-2974, outside the United States at (317) 572-3993, or fax (317) 572-4002.

Wiley publishes in a variety of print and electronic formats and by print-on-demand. Some material included with standard print versions of this book may not be included in e-books or in print-on-demand. If this book refers to media such as a CD or DVD that is not included in the version you purchased, you may download this material at http://booksupport.wiley.com. For more information about Wiley products, visit www.wiley.com.

ISBN 978-1-118-99950-9 (Paperback)
ISBN 978-1-119-02973-1 (ePDF)
ISBN 978-1-119-02977-9 (ePub)

Printed in the United States of America.
V10007433_010919

CONTENTS

FIXED INCOME ANALYSIS WORKBOOK

PART I

LEARNING OBJECTIVES, SUMMARY OVERVIEW, AND PROBLEMS

CHAPTER 1

FIXED-INCOME SECURITIES: DEFINING ELEMENTS

LEARNING OUTCOMES

After completing this chapter, you will be able to do the following:

- describe the basic features of a fixed-income security;
- describe functions of a bond indenture;
- compare affirmative and negative covenants and identify examples of each;
- describe how legal, regulatory, and tax considerations affect the issuance and trading of fixed-income securities;
- describe how cash flows of fixed-income securities are structured;
- describe contingency provisions affecting the timing and/or nature of cash flows of fixed-income securities and identify whether such provisions benefit the borrower or the lender.

SUMMARY OVERVIEW

This chapter provides an introduction to the salient features of fixed-income securities while noting how these features vary among different types of securities. Important points include the following:

- The three important elements that an investor needs to know when investing in a fixed-income security are (1) the bond's features, which determine its scheduled cash flows and thus the bondholder's expected and actual return; (2) the legal, regulatory, and tax considerations that apply to the contractual agreement between the issuer and the bondholders; and (3) the contingency provisions that may affect the bond's scheduled cash flows.
- The basic features of a bond include the issuer, maturity, par value (or principal), coupon rate and frequency, and currency denomination.

- Issuers of bonds include supranational organizations, sovereign governments, non-sovereign governments, quasi-government entities, and corporate issuers.
- Bondholders are exposed to credit risk and may use bond credit ratings to assess the credit quality of a bond.
- A bond's principal is the amount the issuer agrees to pay the bondholder when the bond matures.
- The coupon rate is the interest rate that the issuer agrees to pay to the bondholder each year. The coupon rate can be a fixed rate or a floating rate. Bonds may offer annual, semi-annual, quarterly, or monthly coupon payments depending on the type of bond and where the bond is issued.
- Bonds can be issued in any currency. Bonds such as dual-currency bonds and currency option bonds are connected to two currencies.
- The yield to maturity is the discount rate that equates the present value of the bond's future cash flows until maturity to its price. Yield to maturity can be considered an estimate of the market's expectation for the bond's return.
- A plain vanilla bond has a known cash flow pattern. It has a fixed maturity date and pays a fixed rate of interest over the bond's life.
- The bond indenture or trust deed is the legal contract that describes the form of the bond, the issuer's obligations, and the investor's rights. The indenture is usually held by a financial institution called a trustee, which performs various duties specified in the indenture.
- The issuer is identified in the indenture by its legal name and is obligated to make timely payments of interest and repayment of principal.
- For securitized bonds, the legal obligation to repay bondholders often lies with a separate legal entity—that is, a bankruptcy-remote vehicle that uses the assets as guarantees to back a bond issue.
- How the issuer intends to service the debt and repay the principal should be described in the indenture. The source of repayment proceeds varies depending on the type of bond.
- Collateral backing is a way to alleviate credit risk. Secured bonds are backed by assets or financial guarantees pledged to ensure debt payment. Examples of collateral-backed bonds include collateral trust bonds, equipment trust certificates, mortgage-backed securities, and covered bonds.
- Credit enhancement can be internal or external. Examples of internal credit enhancement include subordination, overcollateralization, and excess spread. A surety bond, a bank guarantee, a letter of credit, and a cash collateral account are examples of external credit enhancement.
- Bond covenants are legally enforceable rules that borrowers and lenders agree on at the time of a new bond issue. Affirmative covenants enumerate what issuers are required to do, whereas negative covenants enumerate what issuers are prohibited from doing.
- An important consideration for investors is where the bonds are issued and traded, because it affects the laws, regulation, and tax status that apply. Bonds issued in a particular country in local currency are domestic bonds if they are issued by entities incorporated in the country and foreign bonds if they are issued by entities incorporated in another country. Eurobonds are issued internationally, outside the jurisdiction of any single country, and are subject to a lower level of listing, disclosure, and regulatory requirements than domestic or foreign bonds. Global bonds are issued in the Eurobond market and at least one domestic market at the same time.
- Although some bonds may offer special tax advantages, as a general rule, interest is taxed at the ordinary income tax rate. Some countries also implement a capital gains tax. There may be specific tax provisions for bonds issued at a discount or bought at a premium.

- An amortizing bond is a bond whose payment schedule requires periodic payment of interest and repayment of principal. This differs from a bullet bond, whose entire payment of principal occurs at maturity. The amortizing bond's outstanding principal amount is reduced to zero by the maturity date for a fully amortized bond, but a balloon payment is required at maturity to retire the bond's outstanding principal amount for a partially amortized bond.
- Sinking fund agreements provide another approach to the periodic retirement of principal, in which an amount of the bond's principal outstanding amount is usually repaid each year throughout the bond's life or after a specified date.
- A floating-rate note or floater is a bond whose coupon is set based on some reference rate plus a spread. FRNs can be floored, capped, or collared. An inverse FRN is a bond whose coupon has an inverse relationship to the reference rate.
- Other coupon payment structures include bonds with step-up coupons, which pay coupons that increase by specified amounts on specified dates; bonds with credit-linked coupons, which change when the issuer's credit rating changes; bonds with payment-in-kind coupons that allow the issuer to pay coupons with additional amounts of the bond issue rather than in cash; and bonds with deferred coupons, which pay no coupons in the early years following the issue but higher coupons thereafter.
- The payment structures for index-linked bonds vary considerably among countries. A common index-linked bond is an inflation-linked bond or linker whose coupon payments and/or principal repayments are linked to a price index. Index-linked payment structures include zero-coupon-indexed bonds, interest-indexed bonds, capital-indexed bonds, and indexed-annuity bonds.
- Common types of bonds with embedded options include callable bonds, putable bonds, and convertible bonds. These options are "embedded" in the sense that there are provisions provided in the indenture that grant either the issuer or the bondholder certain rights affecting the disposal or redemption of the bond. They are not separately traded securities.
- Callable bonds give the issuer the right to buy bonds back prior to maturity, thereby raising the reinvestment risk for the bondholder. For this reason, callable bonds have to offer a higher yield and sell at a lower price than otherwise similar non-callable bonds to compensate the bondholders for the value of the call option to the issuer.
- Putable bonds give the bondholder the right to sell bonds back to the issuer prior to maturity. Putable bonds offer a lower yield and sell at a higher price than otherwise similar non-putable bonds to compensate the issuer for the value of the put option to the bondholders.
- A convertible bond gives the bondholder the right to convert the bond into common shares of the issuing company. Because this option favors the bondholder, convertible bonds offer a lower yield and sell at a higher price than otherwise similar non-convertible bonds.

PROBLEMS

This question set was developed by Lee M. Dunham, CFA (Omaha, NE, USA), and Elbie Louw, CFA, CIPM (Pretoria, South Africa). Copyright © 2013 CFA Institute.

1. A 10-year bond was issued four years ago. The bond is denominated in US dollars, offers a coupon rate of 10% with interest paid semi-annually, and is currently priced at 102% of par. The bond's:
   A. tenor is six years.
   B. nominal rate is 5%.
   C. redemption value is 102% of the par value.

2. A sovereign bond has a maturity of 15 years. The bond is *best* described as a:
   A. perpetual bond.
   B. pure discount bond.
   C. capital market security.
3. A company has issued a floating-rate note with a coupon rate equal to the three-month Libor + 65 basis points. Interest payments are made quarterly on 31 March, 30 June, 30 September, and 31 December. On 31 March and 30 June, the three-month Libor is 1.55% and 1.35%, respectively. The coupon rate for the interest payment made on 30 June is:
   A. 2.00%.
   B. 2.10%.
   C. 2.20%.
4. The legal contract that describes the form of the bond, the obligations of the issuer, and the rights of the bondholders can be *best* described as a bond's:
   A. covenant.
   B. indenture.
   C. debenture.
5. Which of the following is a type of external credit enhancement?
   A. Covenants
   B. A surety bond
   C. Overcollaterization
6. An affirmative covenant is *most likely* to stipulate:
   A. limits on the issuer's leverage ratio.
   B. how the proceeds of the bond issue will be used.
   C. the maximum percentage of the issuer's gross assets that can be sold.
7. Which of the following *best* describes a negative bond covenant? The issuer is:
   A. required to pay taxes as they come due.
   B. prohibited from investing in risky projects.
   C. required to maintain its current lines of business.
8. A South African company issues bonds denominated in pound sterling that are sold to investors in the United Kingdom. These bonds can be *best* described as:
   A. Eurobonds.
   B. global bonds.
   C. foreign bonds.
9. Relative to domestic and foreign bonds, Eurobonds are *most likely* to be:
   A. bearer bonds.
   B. registered bonds.
   C. subject to greater regulation.
10. An investor in a country with an original issue discount tax provision purchases a 20-year zero-coupon bond at a deep discount to par value. The investor plans to hold the bond until the maturity date. The investor will *most likely* report:
    A. a capital gain at maturity.
    B. a tax deduction in the year the bond is purchased.
    C. taxable income from the bond every year until maturity.
11. A bond that is characterized by a fixed periodic payment schedule that reduces the bond's outstanding principal amount to zero by the maturity date is *best* described as a:
    A. bullet bond.
    B. plain vanilla bond.
    C. fully amortized bond.

12. If interest rates are expected to increase, the coupon payment structure *most likely* to benefit the issuer is a:
    A. step-up coupon.
    B. inflation-linked coupon.
    C. cap in a floating-rate note.
13. Investors who believe that interest rates will rise *most likely* prefer to invest in:
    A. inverse floaters.
    B. fixed-rate bonds.
    C. floating-rate notes.
14. A 10-year, capital-indexed bond linked to the Consumer Price Index (CPI) is issued with a coupon rate of 6% and a par value of 1,000. The bond pays interest semi-annually. During the first six months after the bond's issuance, the CPI increases by 2%. On the first coupon payment date, the bond's:
    A. coupon rate increases to 8%.
    B. coupon payment is equal to 40.
    C. principal amount increases to 1,020.
15. The provision that provides bondholders the right to sell the bond back to the issuer at a predetermined price prior to the bond's maturity date is referred to as:
    A. a put provision.
    B. a make-whole call provision.
    C. an original issue discount provision.
16. Which of the following provisions is a benefit to the issuer?
    A. Put provision
    B. Call provision
    C. Conversion provision
17. Relative to an otherwise similar option-free bond, a:
    A. putable bond will trade at a higher price.
    B. callable bond will trade at a higher price.
    C. convertible bond will trade at a lower price.

CHAPTER 2

FIXED-INCOME MARKETS: ISSUANCE, TRADING, AND FUNDING

LEARNING OUTCOMES

After completing this chapter, you will be able to do the following:

- describe classifications of global fixed-income markets;
- describe the use of interbank offered rates as reference rates in floating-rate debt;
- describe mechanisms available for issuing bonds in primary markets;
- describe secondary markets for bonds;
- describe securities issued by sovereign governments, non-sovereign governments, government agencies, and supranational entities;
- describe types of debt issued by corporations;
- describe short-term funding alternatives available to banks;
- describe repurchase agreements (repos) and their importance to investors who borrow short term.

SUMMARY OVERVIEW

Debt financing is an important source of funds for governments, government-related entities, financial institutions, and non-financial companies. Well-functioning fixed-income markets help ensure that capital is allocated efficiently to its highest and best use globally. Important points include the following:

- The most widely used ways of classifying fixed-income markets include the type of issuer; the bonds' credit quality, maturity, currency denomination, and type of coupon; and where the bonds are issued and traded.

- Based on the type of issuer, the three major bond market sectors are the government and government-related sector, the corporate sector, and the structured finance sector. The major issuers of bonds globally are governments and financial institutions.
- Investors make a distinction between investment-grade and high-yield bond markets based on the issuer's credit quality.
- Money markets are where securities with original maturities ranging from overnight to one year are issued and traded, whereas capital markets are where securities with original maturities longer than one year are issued and traded.
- The majority of bonds are denominated in either euros or US dollars.
- Investors make a distinction between bonds that pay a fixed rate versus a floating rate of interest. The coupon rate of floating-rate bonds is expressed as a reference rate plus a spread. Interbank offered rates, such as Libor, are the most commonly used reference rates for floating-rate debt and other financial instruments.
- Interbank offered rates are sets of rates that reflect the rates at which banks believe they could borrow unsecured funds from other banks in the interbank market for different currencies and different maturities.
- Based on where the bonds are issued and traded, a distinction is made between domestic and international bond markets. The latter includes the Eurobond market, which falls outside the jurisdiction of any single country and is characterized by less reporting, regulatory, and tax constraints. Investors also make a distinction between developed and emerging bond markets.
- Fixed-income indices are used by investors and investment managers to describe bond markets or sectors and to evaluate performance of investments and investment managers.
- The largest investors in bonds include central banks; institutional investors, such as pension funds, some hedge funds, charitable foundations and endowments, insurance companies, and banks; and retail investors.
- Primary markets are markets in which issuers first sell bonds to investors to raise capital. Secondary markets are markets in which existing bonds are subsequently traded among investors.
- There are two mechanisms for issuing a bond in primary markets: a public offering, in which any member of the public may buy the bonds, or a private placement, in which only an investor or small group of investors may buy the bonds either directly from the issuer or through an investment bank.
- Public bond issuing mechanisms include underwritten offerings, best effort offerings, shelf registrations, and auctions.
- When an investment bank underwrites a bond issue, it buys the entire issue and takes the risk of reselling it to investors or dealers. In contrast, in a best efforts offering, the investment bank serves only as a broker and sells the bond issue only if it is able to do so. Underwritten and best effort offerings are frequently used in the issuance of corporate bonds.
- The underwriting process typically includes six phases: the determination of the funding needs, the selection of the underwriter, the structuring and announcement of the bond offering, pricing, issuance, and closing.
- A shelf registration is a method for issuing securities in which the issuer files a single document with regulators that describes a range of future issuances.
- An auction is a public offering method that involves bidding, and that is helpful in providing price discovery and in allocating securities. It is frequently used in the issuance of sovereign bonds.
- Most bonds are traded in over-the-counter (OTC) markets, and institutional investors are the major buyers and sellers of bonds in secondary markets.

- Sovereign bonds are issued by national governments primarily for fiscal reasons. They take different names and forms depending on where they are issued, their maturities, and their coupon types. Most sovereign bonds are fixed-rate bonds, although some national governments also issue floating-rate bonds and inflation-linked bonds.
- Local governments, quasi-government entities, and supranational agencies issue bonds, which are named non-sovereign, quasi-government, and supranational bonds, respectively.
- Companies raise debt in the form of bilateral loans, syndicated loans, commercial paper, notes, and bonds.
- Commercial paper is a short-term unsecured security that is used by companies as a source of short-term and bridge financing. Investors in commercial paper are exposed to credit risk, although defaults are rare. Many issuers roll over their commercial paper on a regular basis.
- Corporate bonds and notes take different forms depending on the maturities, coupon payment, and principal repayment structures. Important considerations also include collateral backing and contingency provisions.
- Medium-term notes are securities that are offered continuously to investors by an agent of the issuer. They can have short-term or long-term maturities.
- Financial institutions have access to additional sources of funds, such as retail deposits, central bank funds, interbank funds, large-denomination negotiable certificates of deposit, and repurchase agreements.
- A repurchase agreement is similar to a collateralized loan. It involves the sale of a security (the collateral) with a simultaneous agreement by the seller (the borrower) to buy the same security back from the purchaser (the lender) at an agreed-on price in the future. Repurchase agreements are a common source of funding for dealer firms and are also used to borrow securities to implement short positions.

PROBLEMS

This question set was developed by Michael Whitehurst, CFA (San Diego, CA, USA). Copyright © 2013 by CFA Institute.

1. In most countries, the bond market sector with the smallest amount of bonds outstanding is *most likely* the:
   A. government sector.
   B. financial corporate sector.
   C. non-financial corporate sector.
2. The distinction between investment grade debt and non-investment grade debt is *best* described by differences in:
   A. tax status.
   B. credit quality.
   C. maturity dates.
3. A bond issued internationally, outside the jurisdiction of the country in whose currency the bond is denominated, is *best* described as a:
   A. Eurobond.
   B. foreign bond.
   C. municipal bond.

4. Compared with developed markets bonds, emerging markets bonds *most likely*:
   A. offer lower yields.
   B. exhibit higher risk.
   C. benefit from lower growth prospects.
5. With respect to floating-rate bonds, a reference rate such as the London interbank offered rate (Libor) is *most likely* used to determine the bond's:
   A. spread.
   B. coupon rate.
   C. frequency of coupon payments.
6. Which of the following statements is *most accurate*? An interbank offered rate:
   A. is a single reference rate.
   B. applies to borrowing periods of up to 10 years.
   C. is used as a reference rate for interest rate swaps.
7. An investment bank that underwrites a bond issue *most likely*:
   A. buys and resells the newly issued bonds to investors or dealers.
   B. acts as a broker and receives a commission for selling the bonds to investors.
   C. incurs less risk associated with selling the bonds than in a best efforts offering.
8. In major developed bond markets, newly issued sovereign bonds are *most* often sold to the public via a(n):
   A. auction.
   B. private placement.
   C. best efforts offering.
9. A mechanism by which an issuer may be able to offer additional bonds to the general public without preparing a new and separate offering circular *best* describes:
   A. the grey market.
   B. a shelf registration.
   C. a private placement.
10. Which of the following statements related to secondary bond markets is *most accurate*?
    A. Newly issued corporate bonds are issued in secondary bond markets.
    B. Secondary bond markets are where bonds are traded between investors.
    C. The major participants in secondary bond markets globally are retail investors.
11. A bond market in which a communications network matches buy and sell orders initiated from various locations is *best* described as an:
    A. organized exchange.
    B. open market operation.
    C. over-the-counter market.
12. A liquid secondary bond market allows an investor to sell a bond at:
    A. the desired price.
    B. a price at least equal to the purchase price.
    C. a price close to the bond's fair market value.
13. Sovereign bonds are *best* described as:
    A. bonds issued by local governments.
    B. secured obligations of a national government.
    C. bonds backed by the taxing authority of a national government.
14. Agency bonds are issued by:
    A. local governments.
    B. national governments.
    C. quasi-government entities.

15. The type of bond issued by a multilateral agency such as the International Monetary Fund (IMF) is *best* described as a:
    A. sovereign bond.
    B. supranational bond.
    C. quasi-government bond.
16. Which of the following statements relating to commercial paper is *most accurate*?
    A. There is no secondary market for trading commercial paper.
    B. Only the strongest, highly rated companies issue commercial paper.
    C. Commercial paper is a source of interim financing for long-term projects.
17. Eurocommerical paper is *most likely*:
    A. negotiable.
    B. denominated in euro.
    C. issued on a discount basis.
18. When issuing debt, a company may use a sinking fund arrangement as a means of reducing:
    A. credit risk.
    B. inflation risk.
    C. interest rate risk.
19. Which of the following is a source of wholesale funds for banks?
    A. Demand deposits
    B. Money market accounts
    C. Negotiable certificates of deposit
20. A characteristic of negotiable certificates of deposit is:
    A. they are mostly available in small denominations.
    B. they can be sold in the open market prior to maturity.
    C. a penalty is imposed if the depositor withdraws funds prior to maturity.
21. A repurchase agreement is *most* comparable to a(n):
    A. interbank deposit.
    B. collateralized loan.
    C. negotiable certificate of deposit.
22. The repo margin on a repurchase agreement is *most likely* to be lower when:
    A. the underlying collateral is in short supply.
    B. the maturity of the repurchase agreement is long.
    C. the credit risk associated with the underlying collateral is high.

CHAPTER 3

INTRODUCTION TO FIXED-INCOME VALUATION

LEARNING OUTCOMES

After completing this chapter, you will be able to do the following:

- calculate a bond's price given a market discount rate;
- identify the relationships among a bond's price, coupon rate, maturity, and market discount rate (yield-to-maturity);
- define spot rates and calculate the price of a bond using spot rates;
- describe and calculate the flat price, accrued interest, and the full price of a bond;
- describe matrix pricing;
- calculate and interpret yield measures for fixed-rate bonds, floating-rate notes, and money market instruments;
- define and compare the spot curve, yield curve on coupon bonds, par curve, and forward curve;
- define forward rates and calculate spot rates from forward rates, forward rates from spot rates, and the price of a bond using forward rates;
- compare, calculate, and interpret yield spread measures.

SUMMARY OVERVIEW

This chapter covers the principles and techniques that are used in the valuation of fixed-rate bonds, as well as floating-rate notes and money market instruments. These building blocks are used extensively in fixed-income analysis. The following are the main points made in the chapter:

- The market discount rate is the rate of return required by investors given the risk of the investment in the bond.

- A bond is priced at a premium above par value when the coupon rate is greater than the market discount rate.
- A bond is priced at a discount below par value when the coupon rate is less than the market discount rate.
- The amount of any premium or discount is the present value of the "excess" or "deficiency" in the coupon payments relative to the yield-to-maturity.
- The yield-to-maturity, the internal rate of return on the cash flows, is the implied market discount rate given the price of the bond.
- A bond price moves inversely with its market discount rate.
- The relationship between a bond price and its market discount rate is convex.
- The price of a lower-coupon bond is more volatile than the price of a higher-coupon bond, other things being equal.
- Generally, the price of a longer-term bond is more volatile than the price of shorter-term bond, other things being equal. An exception to this phenomenon can occur on low-coupon (but not zero-coupon) bonds that are priced at a discount to par value.
- Assuming no default, premium and discount bond prices are "pulled to par" as maturity nears.
- A spot rate is the yield-to-maturity on a zero-coupon bond.
- A yield-to-maturity can be approximated as a weighted average of the underlying spot rates.
- Between coupon dates, the full (or invoice, or "dirty") price of a bond is split between the flat (or quoted, or "clean") price and the accrued interest.
- Flat prices are quoted to not misrepresent the daily increase in the full price as a result of interest accruals.
- Accrued interest is calculated as a proportional share of the next coupon payment using either the actual/actual or 30/360 methods to count days.
- Matrix pricing is used to value illiquid bonds by using prices and yields on comparable securities having the same or similar credit risk, coupon rate, and maturity.
- The periodicity of an annual interest rate is the number of periods in the year.
- A yield quoted on a semiannual bond basis is an annual rate for a periodicity of two. It is the yield per semiannual period times two.
- The general rule for periodicity conversions is that compounding more frequently at a lower annual rate corresponds to compounding less frequently at a higher annual rate.
- Street convention yields assume payments are made on scheduled dates, neglecting weekends and holidays.
- The current yield is the annual coupon payment divided by the flat price, thereby neglecting as a measure of the investor's rate of return the time value of money, any accrued interest, and the gain from buying at a discount and the loss from buying at a premium.
- The simple yield is like the current yield but includes the straight-line amortization of the discount or premium.
- The yield-to-worst on a callable bond is the lowest of the yield-to-first-call, yield-to-second-call, and so on, calculated using the call price for the future value and the call date for the number of periods.
- The option-adjusted yield on a callable bond is the yield-to-maturity after adding the theoretical value of the call option to the price.
- A floating-rate note (floater, or FRN) maintains a more stable price than a fixed-rate note because interest payments adjust for changes in market interest rates.
- The quoted margin on a floater is typically the specified yield spread over or under the reference rate, which often is Libor.

- The discount margin on a floater is the spread required by investors, and to which the quoted margin must be set, for the FRN to trade at par value on a rate reset date.
- Money market instruments, having one year or less time-to-maturity, are quoted on a discount rate or add-on rate basis.
- Money market discount rates understate the investor's rate of return (and the borrower's cost of funds) because the interest income is divided by the face value or the total amount redeemed at maturity, and not by the amount of the investment.
- Money market instruments need to be converted to a common basis for analysis.
- A money market bond equivalent yield is an add-on rate for a 365-day year.
- The periodicity of a money market instrument is the number of days in the year divided by the number of days to maturity. Therefore, money market instruments with different times-to-maturity have annual rates for different periodicities.
- In theory, the maturity structure, or term structure, of interest rates is the relationship between yields-to-maturity and times-to-maturity on bonds having the same currency, credit risk, liquidity, tax status, and periodicity.
- A spot curve is a series of yields-to-maturity on zero-coupon bonds.
- A frequently used yield curve is a series of yields-to-maturity on coupon bonds.
- A par curve is a series of yields-to-maturity assuming the bonds are priced at par value.
- In a cash market, the delivery of the security and cash payment is made on a settlement date within a customary time period after the trade date—for example, "T + 3."
- In a forward market, the delivery of the security and cash payment is made on a predetermined future date.
- A forward rate is the interest rate on a bond or money market instrument traded in a forward market.
- An implied forward rate (or forward yield) is the breakeven reinvestment rate linking the return on an investment in a shorter-term zero-coupon bond to the return on an investment in a longer-term zero-coupon bond.
- An implied forward curve can be calculated from the spot curve.
- Implied spot rates can be calculated as geometric averages of forward rates.
- A fixed-income bond can be valued using a market discount rate, a series of spot rates, or a series of forward rates.
- A bond yield-to-maturity can be separated into a benchmark and a spread.
- Changes in benchmark rates capture macroeconomic factors that affect all bonds in the market—inflation, economic growth, foreign exchange rates, and monetary and fiscal policy.
- Changes in spreads typically capture microeconomic factors that affect the particular bond—credit risk, liquidity, and tax effects.
- Benchmark rates are usually yields-to-maturity on government bonds or fixed rates on interest rate swaps.
- A G-spread is the spread over or under a government bond rate, and an I-spread is the spread over or under an interest rate swap rate.
- A G-spread or an I-spread can be based on a specific benchmark rate or on a rate interpolated from the benchmark yield curve.
- A Z-spread (zero-volatility spread) is based on the entire benchmark spot curve. It is the constant spread that is added to each spot rate such that the present value of the cash flows matches the price of the bond.
- An option-adjusted spread (OAS) on a callable bond is the Z-spread minus the theoretical value of the embedded call option.

PROBLEMS

This question set was created by Mark Bhasin, CFA (New York, NY), Ryan C. Fuhrmann, CFA (Carmel, IN), Louis Lemos, CFA (Louisville, KY), Susan Ryan, CFA (East Hartland, CT), and Michael Whitehurst, CFA (San Diego, CA). Copyright © 2013 by CFA Institute.

1. A portfolio manager is considering the purchase of a bond with a 5.5% coupon rate that pays interest annually and matures in three years. If the required rate of return on the bond is 5%, the price of the bond per 100 of par value is *closest* to:
   A. 98.65.
   B. 101.36.
   C. 106.43.
2. A bond with two years remaining until maturity offers a 3% coupon rate with interest paid annually. At a market discount rate of 4%, the price of this bond per 100 of par value is *closest* to:
   A. 95.34.
   B. 98.00.
   C. 98.11.
3. An investor who owns a bond with a 9% coupon rate that pays interest semiannually and matures in three years is considering its sale. If the required rate of return on the bond is 11%, the price of the bond per 100 of par value is *closest* to:
   A. 95.00.
   B. 95.11.
   C. 105.15.
4. A bond offers an annual coupon rate of 4%, with interest paid semiannually. The bond matures in two years. At a market discount rate of 6%, the price of this bond per 100 of par value is *closest* to:
   A. 93.07.
   B. 96.28.
   C. 96.33.
5. A bond offers an annual coupon rate of 5%, with interest paid semiannually. The bond matures in seven years. At a market discount rate of 3%, the price of this bond per 100 of par value is *closest* to:
   A. 106.60.
   B. 112.54.
   C. 143.90.
6. A zero-coupon bond matures in 15 years. At a market discount rate of 4.5% per year and assuming annual compounding, the price of the bond per 100 of par value is *closest* to:
   A. 51.30.
   B. 51.67.
   C. 71.62.
7. Consider the following two bonds that pay interest annually:

Bond	Coupon Rate	Time-to-Maturity
A	5%	2 years
B	3%	2 years

At a market discount rate of 4%, the price difference between Bond A and Bond B per 100 of par value is *closest* to:
A. 3.70.
B. 3.77.
C. 4.00.

The following information relates to Questions 8 and 9

Bond	Price	Coupon Rate	Time-to-Maturity
A	101.886	5%	2 years
B	100.000	6%	2 years
C	97.327	5%	3 years

8. Which bond offers the lowest yield-to-maturity?
A. Bond A
B. Bond B
C. Bond C
9. Which bond will *most likely* experience the smallest percent change in price if the market discount rates for all three bonds increase by 100 basis points (bps)?
A. Bond A
B. Bond B
C. Bond C

---

10. Suppose a bond's price is expected to increase by 5% if its market discount rate decreases by 100 bps. If the bond's market discount rate increases by 100 bps, the bond price is *most likely* to change by:
A. 5%.
B. less than 5%.
C. more than 5%.

The following information relates to Questions 11 and 12

Bond	Coupon Rate	Maturity (years)
A	6%	10
B	6%	5
C	8%	5

All three bonds are currently trading at par value.

11. Relative to Bond C, for a 200 basis point decrease in the required rate of return, Bond B will *most likely* exhibit a(n):
A. equal percentage price change.
B. greater percentage price change.
C. smaller percentage price change.

12. Which bond will *most likely* experience the greatest percentage change in price if the market discount rates for all three bonds increase by 100 bps?
    A. Bond A
    B. Bond B
    C. Bond C

---

13. An investor considers the purchase of a 2-year bond with a 5% coupon rate, with interest paid annually. Assuming the sequence of spot rates shown below, the price of the bond is *closest* to:

Time-to-Maturity	Spot Rates
1 year	3%
2 years	4%

    A. 101.93.
    B. 102.85.
    C. 105.81.

14. A 3-year bond offers a 10% coupon rate with interest paid annually. Assuming the following sequence of spot rates, the price of the bond is *closest* to:

Time-to-Maturity	Spot Rates
1 year	8.0%
2 years	9.0%
3 years	9.5%

    A. 96.98.
    B. 101.46.
    C. 102.95.

The following information relates to Questions 15–17

Bond	Coupon Rate	Time-to-Maturity	Time-to-Maturity	Spot Rates
X	8%	3 years	1 year	8%
Y	7%	3 years	2 years	9%
Z	6%	3 years	3 years	10%

All three bonds pay interest annually.

15. Based upon the given sequence of spot rates, the price of Bond X is *closest* to:
    A. 95.02.
    B. 95.28.
    C. 97.63.

16. Based upon the given sequence of spot rates, the price of Bond Y is *closest* to:
    A. 87.50.
    B. 92.54.
    C. 92.76.
17. Based upon the given sequence of spot rates, the yield-to-maturity of Bond Z is *closest* to:
    A. 9.00%.
    B. 9.92%.
    C. 11.93%

---

18. Bond dealers *most* often quote the:
    A. flat price.
    B. full price.
    C. full price plus accrued interest.

The following information relates to Questions 19–21

Bond G, described in the exhibit below, is sold for settlement on 16 June 2014.

Annual Coupon	5%
Coupon Payment Frequency	Semiannual
Interest Payment Dates	10 April and 10 October
Maturity Date	10 October 2016
Day-Count Convention	30/360
Annual Yield-to-Maturity	4%

19. The full price that Bond G will settle at on 16 June 2014 is *closest* to:
    A. 102.36.
    B. 103.10.
    C. 103.65.
20. The accrued interest per 100 of par value for Bond G on the settlement date of 16 June 2014 is *closest* to:
    A. 0.46.
    B. 0.73.
    C. 0.92.
21. The flat price for Bond G on the settlement date of 16 June 2014 is *closest* to:
    A. 102.18.
    B. 103.10.
    C. 104.02.

---

22. Matrix pricing allows investors to estimate market discount rates and prices for bonds:
    A. with different coupon rates.
    B. that are not actively traded.
    C. with different credit quality.

23. When underwriting new corporate bonds, matrix pricing is used to get an estimate of the:
    A. required yield spread over the benchmark rate.
    B. market discount rate of other comparable corporate bonds.
    C. yield-to-maturity on a government bond having a similar time-to-maturity.
24. A bond with 20 years remaining until maturity is currently trading for 111 per 100 of par value. The bond offers a 5% coupon rate with interest paid semiannually. The bond's annual yield-to-maturity is *closest* to:
    A. 2.09%.
    B. 4.18%.
    C. 4.50%.
25. The annual yield-to-maturity, stated for with a periodicity of 12, for a 4-year, zero-coupon bond priced at 75 per 100 of par value is *closest* to:
    A. 6.25%.
    B. 7.21%.
    C. 7.46%.
26. A 5-year, 5% semiannual coupon payment corporate bond is priced at 104.967 per 100 of par value. The bond's yield-to-maturity, quoted on a semiannual bond basis, is 3.897%. An analyst has been asked to convert to a monthly periodicity. Under this conversion, the yield-to-maturity is *closest* to:
    A. 3.87%.
    B. 4.95%.
    C. 7.67%.

The following information relates to Questions 27–30

A bond with 5 years remaining until maturity is currently trading for 101 per 100 of par value. The bond offers a 6% coupon rate with interest paid semiannually. The bond is first callable in 3 years, and is callable after that date on coupon dates according to the following schedule:

End of Year	Call Price
3	102
4	101
5	100

27. The bond's annual yield-to-maturity is *closest* to:
    A. 2.88%.
    B. 5.77%.
    C. 5.94%.
28. The bond's annual yield-to-first-call is *closest* to:
    A. 3.12%.
    B. 6.11%.
    C. 6.25%.
29. The bond's annual yield-to-second-call is *closest* to:
    A. 2.97%.
    B. 5.72%.
    C. 5.94%.

30. The bond's yield-to-worst is *closest* to:
    A. 2.88%.
    B. 5.77%.
    C. 6.25%.
31. A two-year floating-rate note pays 6-month Libor plus 80 bps. The floater is priced at 97 per 100 of par value. Current 6-month Libor is 1.00%. Assume a 30/360 day-count convention and evenly spaced periods. The discount margin for the floater in basis points is *closest* to:
    A. 180 bps.
    B. 236 bps.
    C. 420 bps.
32. An analyst evaluates the following information relating to floating rate notes (FRNs) issued at par value that have 3-month Libor as a reference rate:

Floating Rate Note	Quoted Margin	Discount Margin
X	0.40%	0.32%
Y	0.45%	0.45%
Z	0.55%	0.72%

    Based only on the information provided, the FRN that will be priced at a premium on the next reset date is:
    A. FRN X.
    B. FRN Y.
    C. FRN Z.
33. A 365-day year bank certificate of deposit has an initial principal amount of USD 96.5 million and a redemption amount due at maturity of USD 100 million. The number of days between settlement and maturity is 350. The bond equivalent yield is *closest* to:
    A. 3.48%.
    B. 3.65%.
    C. 3.78%.
34. The bond equivalent yield of a 180-day banker's acceptance quoted at a discount rate of 4.25% for a 360-day year is *closest* to:
    A. 4.31%.
    B. 4.34%.
    C. 4.40%.
35. Which of the following statements describing a par curve is *incorrect*?
    A. A par curve is obtained from a spot curve.
    B. All bonds on a par curve are assumed to have different credit risk.
    C. A par curve is a sequence of yields-to-maturity such that each bond is priced at par value.
36. A yield curve constructed from a sequence of yields-to-maturity on zero-coupon bonds is the:
    A. par curve.
    B. spot curve.
    C. forward curve.

37. The rate, interpreted to be the incremental return for extending the time-to-maturity of an investment for an additional time period, is the:
    A. add-on rate.
    B. forward rate.
    C. yield-to-maturity.

The following information relates to Questions 38 and 39

Time Period	Forward Rate
"0y1y"	0.80%
"1y1y"	1.12%
"2y1y"	3.94%
"3y1y"	3.28%
"4y1y"	3.14%

All rates are annual rates stated for a periodicity of one (effective annual rates).

38. The 3-year implied spot rate is *closest* to:
    A. 1.18%.
    B. 1.94%.
    C. 2.28%.
39. The value per 100 of par value of a two-year, 3.5% coupon bond, with interest payments paid annually, is *closest* to:
    A. 101.58.
    B. 105.01.
    C. 105.82.

---

40. The spread component of a specific bond's yield-to-maturity is *least likely* impacted by changes in:
    A. its tax status.
    B. its quality rating.
    C. inflation in its currency of denomination.
41. The yield spread of a specific bond over the standard swap rate in that currency of the same tenor is *best* described as the:
    A. I-spread.
    B. Z-spread.
    C. G-spread.

The following information relates to Question 42

Bond	Coupon Rate	Time-to-Maturity	Price
UK Government Benchmark Bond	2%	3 years	100.25
UK Corporate Bond	5%	3 years	100.65

Both bonds pay interest annually. The current three-year EUR interest rate swap benchmark is 2.12%.

42. The G-spread in basis points on the UK corporate bond is *closest* to:
    A. 264 bps.
    B. 285 bps.
    C. 300 bps.

---

43. A corporate bond offers a 5% coupon rate and has exactly 3 years remaining to maturity. Interest is paid annually. The following rates are from the benchmark spot curve:

Time-to-Maturity	Spot Rate
1 year	4.86%
2 years	4.95%
3 years	5.65%

The bond is currently trading at a Z-spread of 234 bps. The value of the bond is *closest* to:
    A. 92.38.
    B. 98.35.
    C. 106.56.

44. An option-adjusted spread (OAS) on a callable bond is the Z-spread:
    A. over the benchmark spot curve.
    B. minus the standard swap rate in that currency of the same tenor.
    C. minus the value of the embedded call option expressed in basis points per year.

CHAPTER 4

UNDERSTANDING FIXED-INCOME RISK AND RETURN

LEARNING OUTCOMES

After completing this chapter, you will be able to do the following:

- calculate and interpret the sources of return from investing in a fixed-rate bond;
- define, calculate, and interpret Macaulay, modified, and effective durations;
- explain why effective duration is the most appropriate measure of interest rate risk for bonds with embedded options;
- define key rate duration and describe the key use of key rate durations in measuring the sensitivity of bonds to changes in the shape of the benchmark yield curve;
- explain how a bond's maturity, coupon, embedded options, and yield level affect its interest rate risk;
- calculate the duration of a portfolio and explain the limitations of portfolio duration;
- calculate and interpret the money duration of a bond and price value of a basis point (PVBP);
- calculate and interpret approximate convexity and distinguish between approximate and effective convexity;
- estimate the percentage price change of a bond for a specified change in yield, given the bond's approximate duration and convexity;
- describe how the term structure of yield volatility affects the interest rate risk of a bond;
- describe the relationships among a bond's holding period return, its duration, and the investment horizon;
- explain how changes in credit spread and liquidity affect yield-to-maturity of a bond and how duration and convexity can be used to estimate the price effect of the changes.

SUMMARY OVERVIEW

This chapter covers the risk and return characteristics of fixed-rate bonds. The focus is on the widely used measures of interest rate risk—duration and convexity. These statistics are used extensively in fixed-income analysis. The following are the main points made in the chapter:

- The three sources of return on a fixed-rate bond purchased at par value are (1) receipt of the promised coupon and principal payments on the scheduled dates, (2) reinvestment of coupon payments, and (3) potential capital gains, as well as losses, on the sale of the bond prior to maturity.
- For a bond purchased at a discount or premium, the rate of return also includes the effect of the price being "pulled to par" as maturity nears, assuming no default.
- The total return is the future value of reinvested coupon interest payments and the sale price (or redemption of principal if the bond is held to maturity).
- The horizon yield (or holding period rate of return) is the internal rate of return between the total return and purchase price of the bond.
- Coupon reinvestment risk increases with a higher coupon rate and a longer reinvestment time period.
- Capital gains and losses are measured from the carrying value of the bond and not from the purchase price. The carrying value includes the amortization of the discount or premium if the bond is purchased at a price below or above par value. The carrying value is any point on the constant-yield price trajectory.
- Interest income on a bond is the return associated with the passage of time. Capital gains and losses are the returns associated with a change in the value of a bond as indicated by a change in the yield-to-maturity.
- The two types of interest rate risk on a fixed-rate bond are coupon reinvestment risk and market price risk. These risks offset each other to a certain extent. An investor gains from higher rates on reinvested coupons but loses if the bond is sold at a capital loss because the price is below the constant-yield price trajectory. An investor loses from lower rates on reinvested coupon but gains if the bond is sold at a capital gain because the price is above the constant-yield price trajectory.
- Market price risk dominates coupon reinvestment risk when the investor has a short-term horizon (relative to the time-to-maturity on the bond).
- Coupon reinvestment risk dominates market price risk when the investor has a long-term horizon (relative to the time-to-maturity)—for instance, a buy-and-hold investor.
- Bond duration, in general, measures the sensitivity of the full price (including accrued interest) to a change in interest rates.
- Yield duration statistics measuring the sensitivity of a bond's full price to the bond's own yield-to-maturity include the Macaulay duration, modified duration, money duration, and price value of a basis point.
- Curve duration statistics measuring the sensitivity of a bond's full price to the benchmark yield curve are usually called "effective durations."
- Macaulay duration is the weighted average of the time to receipt of coupon interest and principal payments, in which the weights are the shares of the full price corresponding to each payment. This statistic is annualized by dividing by the periodicity (number of coupon payments or compounding periods in a year).
- Modified duration provides a linear estimate of the percentage price change for a bond given a change in its yield-to-maturity.

- Approximate modified duration approaches modified duration as the change in the yield-to-maturity approaches zero.
- Effective duration is very similar to approximate modified duration. The difference is that approximate modified duration is a yield duration statistic that measures interest rate risk in terms of a change in the bond's own yield-to-maturity, whereas effective duration is a curve duration statistic that measures interest rate risk assuming a parallel shift in the benchmark yield curve.
- Key rate duration is a measure of a bond's sensitivity to a change in the benchmark yield curve at specific maturity segments. Key rate durations can be used to measure a bond's sensitivity to changes in the shape of the yield curve.
- Bonds with an embedded option do not have a meaningful internal rate of return because future cash flows are contingent on interest rates. Therefore, effective duration is the appropriate interest rate risk measure, not modified duration.
- The effective duration of a traditional (option-free) fixed-rate bond is its sensitivity to the benchmark yield curve, which can differ from its sensitivity to its own yield-to-maturity. Therefore, modified duration and effective duration on a traditional (option-free) fixed-rate bond are not necessarily equal.
- During a coupon period, Macaulay and modified durations decline smoothly in a "saw-tooth" pattern, assuming the yield-to-maturity is constant. When the coupon payment is made, the durations jump upward.
- Macaulay and modified durations are inversely related to the coupon rate and the yield-to-maturity.
- Time-to-maturity and Macaulay and modified durations are *usually* positively related. They are *always* positively related on bonds priced at par or at a premium above par value. They are *usually* positively related on bonds priced at a discount below par value. The exception is on long-term, low-coupon bonds, on which it is possible to have a lower duration than on an otherwise comparable shorter-term bond.
- The presence of an embedded call option reduces a bond's effective duration compared with that of an otherwise comparable non-callable bond. The reduction in the effective duration is greater when interest rates are low and the issuer is more likely to exercise the call option.
- The presence of an embedded put option reduces a bond's effective duration compared with that of an otherwise comparable non-putable bond. The reduction in the effective duration is greater when interest rates are high and the investor is more likely to exercise the put option.
- The duration of a bond portfolio can be calculated in two ways: (1) the weighted average of the time to receipt of *aggregate* cash flows and (2) the weighted average of the durations of individual bonds that compose the portfolio.
- The first method to calculate portfolio duration is based on the cash flow yield, which is the internal rate of return on the aggregate cash flows. It cannot be used for bonds with embedded options or for floating-rate notes.
- The second method is simpler to use and quite accurate when the yield curve is relatively flat. Its main limitation is that it assumes a parallel shift in the yield curve in that the yields on all bonds in the portfolio change by the same amount.
- Money duration is a measure of the price change in terms of units of the currency in which the bond is denominated.
- The price value of a basis point (PVBP) is an estimate of the change in the full price of a bond given a 1 bp change in the yield-to-maturity.
- Modified duration is the primary, or first-order, effect on a bond's percentage price change given a change in the yield-to-maturity. Convexity is the secondary, or second-order, effect. It indicates the change in the modified duration as the yield-to-maturity changes.

- Money convexity is convexity times the full price of the bond. Combined with money duration, money convexity estimates the change in the full price of a bond in units of currency given a change in the yield-to-maturity.
- Convexity is a positive attribute for a bond. Other things being equal, a more convex bond appreciates in price more than a less convex bond when yields fall and depreciates less when yields rise.
- Effective convexity is the second-order effect on a bond price given a change in the benchmark yield curve. It is similar to approximate convexity. The difference is that approximate convexity is based on a yield-to-maturity change and effective convexity is based on a benchmark yield curve change.
- Callable bonds have negative effective convexity when interest rates are low. The increase in price when the benchmark yield is reduced is less in absolute value than the decrease in price when the benchmark yield is raised.
- The change in a bond price is the product of (1) the impact per basis-point change in the yield-to-maturity and (2) the number of basis points in the yield change. The first factor is estimated by duration and convexity. The second factor depends on yield volatility.
- The investment horizon is essential in measuring the interest rate risk on a fixed-rate bond.
- For a particular assumption about yield volatility, the Macaulay duration indicates the investment horizon for which coupon reinvestment risk and market price risk offset each other. The assumption is a one-time parallel shift to the yield curve in which the yield-to-maturity and coupon reinvestment rates change by the same amount in the same direction.
- When the investment horizon is greater than the Macaulay duration of the bond, coupon reinvestment risk dominates price risk. The investor's risk is to lower interest rates. The duration gap is negative.
- When the investment horizon is equal to the Macaulay duration of the bond, coupon reinvestment risk offsets price risk. The duration gap is zero.
- When the investment horizon is less than the Macaulay duration of the bond, price risk dominates coupon reinvestment risk. The investor's risk is to higher interest rates. The duration gap is positive.
- Credit risk involves the probability of default and degree of recovery if default occurs, whereas liquidity risk refers to the transaction costs associated with selling a bond.
- For a traditional (option-free) fixed-rate bond, the same duration and convexity statistics apply if a change occurs in the benchmark yield or a change occurs in the spread. The change in the spread can result from a change in credit risk or liquidity risk.
- In practice, there often is interaction between changes in benchmark yields and in the spread over the benchmark.

PROBLEMS

These questions were developed by Danny Hassett, CFA (Cedar Hill, TX, USA), Lou Lemos, CFA (Louisville, KY, USA), and Bin Wang, CFA (Austin, TX, USA). Copyright © 2013 by CFA Institute.

1. A "buy-and-hold" investor purchases a fixed-rate bond at a discount and holds the security until it matures. Which of the following sources of return is *least likely* to contribute to

the investor's total return over the investment horizon, assuming all payments are made as scheduled?

A. Capital gain
B. Principal payment
C. Reinvestment of coupon payments

2. Which of the following sources of return is *most likely* exposed to interest rate risk for an investor of a fixed-rate bond who holds the bond until maturity?
   A. Capital gain or loss
   B. Redemption of principal
   C. Reinvestment of coupon payments
3. An investor purchases a bond at a price above par value. Two years later, the investor sells the bond. The resulting capital gain or loss is measured by comparing the price at which the bond is sold to the:
   A. carrying value.
   B. original purchase price.
   C. original purchase price value plus the amortized amount of the premium.

The following information relates to Problems 4–6

An investor purchases a nine-year, 7% annual coupon payment bond at a price equal to par value. After the bond is purchased and before the first coupon is received, interest rates increase to 8%. The investor sells the bond after five years. Assume that interest rates remain unchanged at 8% over the five-year holding period.

4. Per 100 of par value, the future value of the reinvested coupon payments at the end of the holding period is *closest* to:
   A. 35.00.
   B. 40.26.
   C. 41.07.
5. The capital gain/loss per 100 of par value resulting from the sale of the bond at the end of the five-year holding period is *closest* to a:
   A. loss of 8.45.
   B. loss of 3.31.
   C. gain of 2.75.
6. Assuming that all coupons are reinvested over the holding period, the investor's five-year horizon yield is *closest* to:
   A. 5.66%.
   B. 6.62%.
   C. 7.12%.

---

7. An investor buys a three-year bond with a 5% coupon rate paid annually. The bond, with a yield-to-maturity of 3%, is purchased at a price of 105.657223 per 100 of par value. Assuming a 5-basis point change in yield-to-maturity, the bond's approximate modified duration is *closest* to:
   A. 2.78.
   B. 2.86.
   C. 5.56.

8. Which of the following statements about duration is correct? A bond's:
   A. effective duration is a measure of yield duration.
   B. modified duration is a measure of curve duration.
   C. modified duration cannot be larger than its Macaulay duration.
9. An investor buys a 6% annual payment bond with three years to maturity. The bond has a yield-to-maturity of 8% and is currently priced at 94.845806 per 100 of par. The bond's Macaulay duration is *closest* to:
   A. 2.62.
   B. 2.78.
   C. 2.83.
10. The interest rate risk of a fixed-rate bond with an embedded call option is *best* measured by:
    A. effective duration.
    B. modified duration.
    C. Macaulay duration.
11. Which of the following is *most* appropriate for measuring a bond's sensitivity to shaping risk?
    A. Key rate duration
    B. Effective duration
    C. Modified duration
12. A Canadian pension fund manager seeks to measure the sensitivity of her pension liabilities to market interest rate changes. The manager determines the present value of the liabilities under three interest rate scenarios: a base rate of 7%, a 100 basis-point increase in rates up to 8%, and a 100 basis-point drop in rates down to 6%. The results of the manager's analysis are presented below:

Interest Rate Assumption	Present Value of Liabilities
6%	CAD510.1 million
7%	CAD455.4 million
8%	CAD373.6 million

    The effective duration of the pension fund's liabilities is *closest* to:
    A. 1.49.
    B. 14.99.
    C. 29.97.
13. Which of the following statements about Macaulay duration is correct?
    A. A bond's coupon rate and Macaulay duration are positively related.
    B. A bond's Macaulay duration is inversely related to its yield-to-maturity.
    C. The Macaulay duration of a zero-coupon bond is less than its time-to-maturity.
14. Assuming no change in the credit risk of a bond, the presence of an embedded put option:
    A. reduces the effective duration of the bond.
    B. increases the effective duration of the bond.
    C. does not change the effective duration of the bond.

15. A bond portfolio consists of the following three fixed-rate bonds. Assume annual coupon payments and no accrued interest on the bonds. Prices are per 100 of par value.

Bond	Maturity	Market Value	Price	Coupon	Yield-to-Maturity	Modified Duration
A	6 years	170,000	85.0000	2.00%	4.95%	5.42
B	10 years	120,000	80.0000	2.40%	4.99%	8.44
C	15 years	100,000	100.0000	5.00%	5.00%	10.38

The bond portfolio's modified duration is *closest* to:
A. 7.62.
B. 8.08.
C. 8.20.

16. A limitation of calculating a bond portfolio's duration as the weighted average of the yield durations of the individual bonds that compose the portfolio is that it:
A. assumes a parallel shift to the yield curve.
B. is less accurate when the yield curve is less steeply sloped.
C. is not applicable to portfolios that have bonds with embedded options.

17. Using the information below, which bond has the *greatest* money duration per 100 of par value assuming annual coupon payments and no accrued interest?

Bond	Time-to-Maturity	Price Per 100 of Par Value	Coupon Rate	Yield-to-Maturity	Modified Duration
A	6 years	85.00	2.00%	4.95%	5.42
B	10 years	80.00	2.40%	4.99%	8.44
C	9 years	85.78	3.00%	5.00%	7.54

A. Bond A 
B. Bond B
C. Bond C

18. A bond with exactly nine years remaining until maturity offers a 3% coupon rate with annual coupons. The bond, with a yield-to-maturity of 5%, is priced at 85.784357 per 100 of par value. The estimated price value of a basis point for the bond is *closest* to:
A. 0.0086.
B. 0.0648.
C. 0.1295.

19. The "second-order" effect on a bond's percentage price change given a change in yield-to-maturity can be *best* described as:
A. duration.
B. convexity.
C. yield volatility.

20. A bond is currently trading for 98.722 per 100 of par value. If the bond's yield-to-maturity (YTM) rises by 10 basis points, the bond's full price is expected to fall to 98.669. If the bond's YTM decreases by 10 basis points, the bond's full price is expected to increase to 98.782. The bond's approximate convexity is *closest* to:
    A. 0.071.
    B. 70.906.
    C. 1,144.628.
21. A bond has an annual modified duration of 7.020 and annual convexity of 65.180. If the bond's yield-to-maturity decreases by 25 basis points, the expected percentage price change is *closest* to:
    A. 1.73%.
    B. 1.76%.
    C. 1.78%.
22. A bond has an annual modified duration of 7.140 and annual convexity of 66.200. The bond's yield-to-maturity is expected to increase by 50 basis points. The expected percentage price change is *closest* to:
    A. –3.40%.
    B. –3.49%.
    C. –3.57%.
23. Which of the following statements relating to yield volatility is *most* accurate? If the term structure of yield volatility is downward sloping, then:
    A. short-term rates are higher than long-term rates.
    B. long-term yields are more stable than short-term yields.
    C. short-term bonds will always experience greater price fluctuation than long-term bonds.
24. The holding period for a bond at which the coupon reinvestment risk offsets the market price risk is *best* approximated by:
    A. duration gap.
    B. modified duration.
    C. Macaulay duration.
25. When the investor's investment horizon is less than the Macaulay duration of the bond she owns:
    A. the investor is hedged against interest rate risk.
    B. reinvestment risk dominates, and the investor is at risk of lower rates.
    C. market price risk dominates, and the investor is at risk of higher rates.
26. An investor purchases an annual coupon bond with a 6% coupon rate and exactly 20 years remaining until maturity at a price equal to par value. The investor's investment horizon is eight years. The approximate modified duration of the bond is 11.470 years. The duration gap at the time of purchase is *closest* to:
    A. –7.842.
    B. 3.470.
    C. 4.158.
27. A manufacturing company receives a ratings upgrade and the price increases on its fixed-rate bond. The price increase was *most likely* caused by a(n):
    A. decrease in the bond's credit spread.
    B. increase in the bond's liquidity spread.
    C. increase of the bond's underlying benchmark rate.

CHAPTER 5

FUNDAMENTALS OF CREDIT ANALYSIS

LEARNING OUTCOMES

After completing this chapter, you will be able to do the following:

- describe credit risk and credit-related risks affecting corporate bonds;
- describe default probability and loss severity as components of credit risk;
- describe seniority rankings of corporate debt and explain the potential violation of the priority of claims in a bankruptcy proceeding;
- distinguish between corporate issuer credit ratings and issue credit ratings and describe the rating agency practice of "notching";
- explain risks in relying on ratings from credit rating agencies;
- explain the four Cs (Capacity, Collateral, Covenants, and Character) of traditional credit analysis;
- calculate and interpret financial ratios used in credit analysis;
- evaluate the credit quality of a corporate bond issuer and a bond of that issuer, given key financial ratios of the issuer and the industry;
- describe factors that influence the level and volatility of yield spreads;
- explain special considerations when evaluating the credit of high-yield, sovereign, and non-sovereign government debt issuers and issues.

SUMMARY OVERVIEW

In this chapter, we introduced readers to the basic principles of credit analysis. We described the importance of the credit markets and credit and credit-related risks. We discussed the role and importance of credit ratings and the methodology associated with assigning ratings, as well as the risks of relying on credit ratings. The chapter covered the key components of credit analysis and the financial measure used to help assess creditworthiness.

We also discussed risk versus return when investing in credit and how spread changes affect holding period returns. In addition, we addressed the special considerations to take into account when doing credit analysis of high-yield companies, sovereign borrowers, and non-sovereign government bonds.

- Credit risk is the risk of loss resulting from the borrower failing to make full and timely payments of interest and/or principal.
- The key components of credit risk are risk of default and loss severity in the event of default. The product of the two is expected loss. Investors in higher-quality bonds tend not to focus on loss severity because default risk for those securities is low.
- Loss severity equals (1 – Recovery rate).
- Credit-related risks include downgrade risk (also called credit migration risk) and market liquidity risk. Either of these can cause yield spreads—yield premiums—to rise and bond prices to fall.
- Downgrade risk refers to a decline in an issuer's creditworthiness. Downgrades will cause its bonds to trade with wider yield spreads and thus lower prices.
- Market liquidity risk refers to a widening of the bid–ask spread on an issuer's bonds. Lower-quality bonds tend to have greater market liquidity risk than higher-quality bonds, and during times of market or financial stress, market liquidity risk rises.
- The composition of an issuer's debt and equity is referred to as its "capital structure." Debt ranks ahead of all types of equity with respect to priority of payment, and within the debt component of the capital structure, there can be varying levels of seniority.
- With respect to priority of claims, secured debt ranks ahead of unsecured debt, and within unsecured debt, senior debt ranks ahead of subordinated debt. In the typical case, all of an issuer's bonds have the same probability of default due to cross-default provisions in most indentures. Higher priority of claim implies higher recovery rate—lower loss severity—in the event of default.
- For issuers with more complex corporate structures—for example, a parent holding company that has operating subsidiaries—debt at the holding company is structurally subordinated to the subsidiary debt, although the possibility of more diverse assets and earnings streams from other sources could still result in the parent having higher effective credit quality than a particular subsidiary.
- Recovery rates can vary greatly by issuer and industry. They are influenced by the composition of an issuer's capital structure, where in the economic and credit cycle the default occurred, and what the market's view of the future prospects are for the issuer and its industry.
- The priority of claims in bankruptcy is not always absolute. It can be influenced by several factors, including some leeway accorded to bankruptcy judges, government involvement, or a desire on the part of the more senior creditors to settle with the more junior creditors and allow the issuer to emerge from bankruptcy as a going concern, rather than risking smaller and delayed recovery in the event of a liquidation of the borrower.
- Credit rating agencies, such as Moody's, Standard & Poor's, and Fitch, play a central role in the credit markets. Nearly every bond issued in the broad debt markets carries credit ratings, which are opinions about a bond issue's creditworthiness. Credit ratings enable investors to compare the credit risk of debt issues and issuers within a given industry, across industries, and across geographic markets.
- Bonds rated Aaa to Baa3 by Moody's and AAA to BBB– by Standard & Poor's (S&P) and/or Fitch (higher to lower) are referred to as "investment grade." Bonds rated lower than that—Ba1 or lower by Moody's and BB+ or lower by S&P and/or Fitch—are referred to as "below investment grade" or "speculative grade." Below-investment-grade bonds are also called "high-yield" or "junk" bonds.

- The rating agencies rate both issuers and issues. Issuer ratings are meant to address an issuer's overall creditworthiness—its risk of default. Ratings for issues incorporate such factors as their rankings in the capital structure.
- The rating agencies will notch issue ratings up or down to account for such factors as capital structure ranking for secured or subordinated bonds, reflecting different recovery rates in the event of default. Ratings may also be notched due to structural subordination.
- There are risks in relying too much on credit agency ratings. Creditworthiness may change over time, and initial/current ratings do not necessarily reflect the creditworthiness of an issuer or bond over an investor's holding period. Valuations often adjust before ratings change, and the notching process may not adequately reflect the price decline of a bond that is lower ranked in the capital structure. Because ratings primarily reflect the probability of default but not necessarily the severity of loss given default, bonds with the same rating may have significantly different expected losses (default probability times loss severity). And like analysts, credit rating agencies may have difficulty forecasting certain credit-negative outcomes, such as adverse litigation, leveraging corporate transactions, and such low probability/high severity events as earthquakes and hurricanes.
- The role of corporate credit analysis is to assess the company's ability to make timely payments of interest and to repay principal at maturity.
- Credit analysis is similar to equity analysis. It is important to understand, however, that bonds are contracts and that management's duty to bondholders and other creditors is limited to the terms of the contract. In contrast, management's duty to shareholders is to act in their best interest by trying to maximize the value of the company—perhaps even at the expense of bondholders at times.
- Credit analysts tend to focus more on the downside risk given the asymmetry of risk/return, whereas equity analysts focus more on upside opportunity from earnings growth, and so on.
- The "4 Cs" of credit—capacity, collateral, covenants, and character—provide a useful framework for evaluating credit risk.
- Credit analysis focuses on an issuer's ability to generate cash flow. The analysis starts with an industry assessment—structure and fundamentals—and continues with an analysis of an issuer's competitive position, management strategy, and track record.
- Credit measures are used to calculate an issuer's creditworthiness, as well as to compare its credit quality with peer companies. Key credit ratios focus on leverage and interest coverage and use such measures as EBITDA, free cash flow, funds from operations, interest expense, and balance sheet debt.
- An issuer's ability to access liquidity is also an important consideration in credit analysis.
- The higher the credit risk, the greater the offered/required yield and potential return demanded by investors. Over time, bonds with more credit risk offer higher returns but with greater volatility of return than bonds with lower credit risk.
- The yield on a credit-risky bond comprises the yield on a default risk–free bond with a comparable maturity plus a yield premium, or "spread," that comprises a credit spread and a liquidity premium. That spread is intended to compensate investors for credit risk—risk of default and loss severity in the event of default—and the credit-related risks that can cause spreads to widen and prices to decline—downgrade or credit migration risk and market liquidity risk.

$$\text{Yield spread} = \text{Liquidity premium} + \text{Credit spread}$$

- In times of financial market stress, the liquidity premium can increase sharply, causing spreads to widen on all credit-risky bonds, with lower-quality issuers most affected. In times of credit improvement or stability, however, credit spreads can narrow sharply as well, providing attractive investment returns.

- Credit curves—the plot of yield spreads for a given bond issuer across the yield curve—are typically upward sloping, with the exception of high premium-priced bonds and distressed bonds, where credit curves can be inverted because of the fear of default, when all creditors at a given ranking in the capital structure will receive the same recovery rate without regard to debt maturity.
- The impact of spread changes on holding period returns for credit-risky bonds are a product of two primary factors: the basis point spread change and the sensitivity of price to yield as reflected by (end-of-period) modified duration and convexity. Spread narrowing enhances holding period returns, whereas spread widening has a negative impact on holding period returns. Longer-duration bonds have greater price and return sensitivity to changes in spread than shorter-duration bonds.

$$\text{Price impact} \approx -(\text{MDur} \times \Delta\text{Spread}) + \tfrac{1}{2}\text{Cvx} \times (\Delta\text{Spread})^2$$

- For high-yield bonds, with their greater risk of default, more emphasis should be placed on an issuer's sources of liquidity, as well as on its debt structure and corporate structure. Credit risk can vary greatly across an issuer's debt structure depending on the seniority ranking. Many high-yield companies have complex capital structures, resulting in different levels of credit risk depending on where the debt resides.
- Covenant analysis is especially important for high-yield bonds. Key covenants include payment restrictions, limitation on liens, change of control, coverage maintenance tests (often limited to bank loans), and any guarantees from restricted subsidiaries. Covenant language can be very technical and legalistic, so it may help to seek legal or expert assistance.
- An equity-like approach to high-yield analysis can be helpful. Calculating and comparing enterprise value with EBITDA and debt/EBITDA can show a level of equity "cushion" or support beneath an issuer's debt.
- Sovereign credit analysis includes assessing an issuer's ability and willingness to pay its debt obligations. Willingness to pay is important because, due to sovereign immunity, a sovereign government cannot be forced to pay its debts.
- In assessing sovereign credit risk, a helpful framework is to focus on five broad areas: (1) institutional effectiveness and political risks; (2) economic structure and growth prospects; (3) external liquidity and international investment position; (4) fiscal performance, flexibility, and debt burden; and (5) monetary flexibility.
- Among the characteristics of a high-quality sovereign credit are the absence of corruption and/or challenges to political framework; governmental checks and balances; respect for rule of law and property rights; commitment to honor debts; high per capita income with stable, broad-based growth prospects; control of a reserve or actively traded currency; currency flexibility; low foreign debt and foreign financing needs relative to receipts in foreign currencies; stable or declining ratio of debt to GDP; low debt service as a percent of revenue; low ratio of net debt to GDP; operationally independent central bank; track record of low and stable inflation; and a well-developed banking system and active money market.
- Non-sovereign or local government bonds, including municipal bonds, are typically either general obligation bonds or revenue bonds.
- General obligation (GO) bonds are backed by the taxing authority of the issuing non-sovereign government. The credit analysis of GO bonds has some similarities to sovereign analysis—debt burden per capita versus income per capita, tax burden, demographics, and economic

diversity. Underfunded and "off-balance-sheet" liabilities, such as pensions for public employees and retirees, are debt-like in nature.

- Revenue-backed bonds support specific projects, such as toll roads, bridges, airports, and other infrastructure. The creditworthiness comes from the revenues generated by usage fees and tolls levied.

PROBLEMS

1. The risk that a bond's creditworthiness declines is *best* described by:
   A. credit migration risk.
   B. market liquidity risk.
   C. spread widening risk.
2. Stedsmart Ltd and Fignermo Ltd are alike with respect to financial and operating characteristics, except that Stedsmart Ltd has less publicly traded debt outstanding than Fignermo Ltd. Stedsmart Ltd is *most likely* to have:
   A. no market liquidity risk.
   B. lower market liquidity risk.
   C. higher market liquidity risk.
3. In the event of default, debentures' claims will *most likely* rank:
   A. above that of secured debt holders.
   B. below that of secured debt holders.
   C. the same as that of secured debt holders.
4. In the event of default, the recovery rate of which of the following bonds would *most likely* be the highest?
   A. First mortgage debt
   B. Senior unsecured debt
   C. Junior subordinate debt
5. During bankruptcy proceedings of a firm, the priority of claims was not strictly adhered to. Which of the following is the *least likely* explanation for this outcome?
   A. Senior creditors compromised.
   B. The value of secured assets was less than the amount of the claims.
   C. A judge's order resulted in actual claims not adhering to strict priority of claims.
6. A fixed income analyst is *least likely* to conduct an independent analysis of credit risk because credit rating agencies:
   A. may at times mis-rate issues.
   B. often lag the market in pricing credit risk.
   C. cannot foresee future debt-financed acquisitions.
7. If goodwill makes up a large percentage of a company's total assets, this *most likely* indicates that:
   A. the company has low free cash flow before dividends.
   B. there is a low likelihood that the market price of the company's common stock is below book value.
   C. a large percentage of the company's assets are not of high quality.
8. In order to analyze the **collateral** of a company a credit analyst should assess the:
   A. cash flows of the company.
   B. soundness of management's strategy.
   C. value of the company's assets in relation to the level of debt.

9. In order to determine the **capacity** of a company, it would be *most* appropriate to analyze the:
   A. company's strategy.
   B. growth prospects of the industry.
   C. aggressiveness of the company's accounting policies.
10. A credit analyst is evaluating the credit worthiness of three companies: a construction company, a travel and tourism company, and a beverage company. Both the construction and travel and tourism companies are cyclical, whereas the beverage company is non-cyclical. The construction company has the highest debt level of the three companies. The highest credit risk is *most likely* exhibited by the:
    A. construction company.
    B. beverage company.
    C. travel and tourism company.
11. Based on the information provided in Exhibit 1, the EBITDA interest coverage ratio of Adidas AG is *closest* to:
    A. 7.91x.
    B. 10.12x.
    C. 12.99x.

EXHIBIT 1 Adidas AG Excerpt from Consolidated Income Statement Year Ending 31 December 2010 (€ in millions)

Gross Profit	5,730
Royalty and commission income	100
Other operating income	110
Other operating expenses	5,046
Operating profit	894
Interest income	25
Interest expense	113
Income before taxes	806
Income taxes	238
Net income	568
Additional information:	
Depreciation and amortization: €249 million	

Source: Adidas AG Annual Financial Statements, December 2010

12. The following information is from the annual report of Adidas AG for December 2010:
    - Depreciation and amortization: €249 million
    - Total assets: €10,618 million
    - Total debt: €1,613 million
    - Shareholders' equity: €4,616 million

    The debt/capital ratio of Adidas AG is *closest* to:
    A. 15.19%.
    B. 25.90%.
    C. 34.94%.

13. Funds from operations (FFO) of Pay Handle Ltd increased in 2011. In 2011 the total debt of the company remained unchanged, while additional common shares were issued. Pay Handle Ltd's ability to service its debt in 2011, as compared to 2010, *most likely*:
    A. improved.
    B. worsened.
    C. remained the same.
14. Based on the information in Exhibit 2, Grupa Zywiec SA's credit risk is *most likely*:
    A. lower than the industry.
    B. higher than the industry.
    C. the same as the industry.

EXHIBIT 2 European Food, Beverage, and Tobacco Industry and Grupa Zywiec SA Selected Financial Ratios for 2010

	Total Debt/Total Capital (%)	FFO/Total Debt (%)	Return on Capital (%)	Total Debt/ EBITDA (x)	EBITDA Interest Coverage (x)
Grupa Zywiec SA	47.1	77.5	19.6	1.2	17.7
Industry Median	**42.4**	**23.6**	**6.55**	**2.85**	**6.45**

15. Based on the information in Exhibit 3, the credit rating of Davide Campari-Milano S.p.A. is *most likely*:
    A. lower than Associated British Foods plc.
    B. higher than Associated British Foods plc.
    C. the same as Associated British Foods plc.

EXHIBIT 3 European Food, Beverage, and Tobacco Industry; Associated British Foods plc; and Davide Campari-Milano S.p.A Selected Financial Ratios, 2010

Company	Total Debt/Total Capital (%)	FFO/ Total Debt (%)	Return on Capital (%)	Total Debt/ EBITDA (x)	EBITDA Interest Coverage (x)
Associated British Foods plc	0.2	84.3	0.1	1.0	13.9
Davide Campari-Milano S.p.A.	42.9	22.9	8.2	3.2	3.2
European Food, Beverage, and Tobacco Median	**42.4**	**23.6**	**6.55**	**2.85**	**6.45**

16. Holding all other factors constant, the *most likely* effect of low demand and heavy new issue supply on bond yield spreads is that yield spreads will:
    A. widen.
    B. tighten.
    C. not be affected.

CHAPTER 6

CREDIT ANALYSIS MODELS

LEARNING OUTCOMES

After completing this chapter, you will be able to do the following:

- explain probability of default, loss given default, expected loss, and present value of the expected loss, and describe the relative importance of each across the credit spectrum;
- explain credit scoring and credit ratings, including why they are called ordinal rankings;
- explain strengths and weaknesses of credit ratings;
- explain structural models of corporate credit risk, including why equity can be viewed as a call option on the company's assets;
- explain reduced form models of corporate credit risk, including why debt can be valued as the sum of expected discounted cash flows after adjusting for risk;
- explain assumptions, strengths, and weaknesses of both structural and reduced form models of corporate credit risk;
- explain the determinants of the term structure of credit spreads;
- calculate and interpret the present value of the expected loss on a bond over a given time horizon;
- compare the credit analysis required for asset-backed securities to analysis of corporate debt.

SUMMARY OVERVIEW

Credit risk analysis is extremely important to a well-functioning economy. Financial crises often originate in the mis-measuring of, and changes in, credit risk. Mis-rating can result in mispricing and misallocation of resources. This chapter discusses a variety of approaches to credit risk analysis: credit scoring, credit rating, structural models, and reduced form models. In addition, the chapter discusses asset-backed securities and explains why using approaches designed for credit risk analysis of debt may result in problematic measures. Key points of the chapter include the following:

- There are four credit risk measures of a bond: the probability of default, the loss given default, the expected loss, and the present value of the expected loss. Of the four, the present value of the expected loss is the most important because it represents the highest price one is willing to pay to own the bond and, as such, it incorporates an adjustment for risk and the time value of money.

- Credit scoring and credit ratings are traditional approaches to credit risk assessment, used to rank retail borrowers versus companies, governments, and structured products.
- During the financial crisis, credit-rating agencies mis-rated debt issues, generating concern over the method in which credit-rating agencies are paid for their services.
- Structural models of credit risk assume a simple balance sheet for the company consisting of a single liability, a zero-coupon bond. Structural models also assume the assets of the company trade and are observable.
- In a structural model, the company's equity can be viewed as a European call option on the assets of the company, with a strike price equal to the debt's face value. This analogy is useful for understanding the debt's probability of default, its loss given default, its expected loss, and the present value of the expected loss.
- The structural model's inputs can only be estimated using calibration, where the inputs are inferred from market prices of the company's equity.
- Reduced form models of credit risk consider a company's traded liabilities. Reduced form models also assume a given process for the company's default time and loss given default. Both of these quantities can depend on the state of the economy as captured by a collection of macroeconomic factors.
- Using option pricing methodology, reduced form models provide insights into the debt's expected loss and the present value of the expected loss.
- The reduced form model's inputs can be estimated using either calibration or historical estimation. Historical estimation is the preferred methodology; it incorporates past time-series observations of company defaults, macroeconomic variables, and company balance sheet characteristics. Hazard rate estimation techniques are used in this regard.
- The term structure of credit spreads is the difference between yields on risky bonds versus default-free zero-coupon bonds. These yields can be estimated from the market prices of traded coupon bonds of both types.
- The present value of the expected loss on any bond can be estimated using the term structure of credit spreads.
- Asset-backed securities (ABS) are liabilities issued by a special purpose vehicle (SPV). The SPV's assets, called a collateral pool, consist of a collection of loans. To finance its assets, the SPV issues bonds (the ABS) in tranches that have different priorities with respect to cash flows and losses, called the waterfall.
- ABS do not default, but they can lose value as the SPV's collateral pool incurs defaults. Modeling an ABS's credit risk—the probability of loss, the loss given default, the expected loss, and the present value of the loss—is a complex exercise.

PROBLEMS

This question set was developed by Don Taylor, CFA (Chadds Ford, PA, USA). Copyright © 2013 by CFA Institute.

Campbell Fixed Income Analytics provides credit analysis services on a consulting basis to fixed income managers. A new hire, Liam Cassidy, has been asked by his supervisor, Malcolm

Moriarty, to answer some questions and to analyze a corporate bond issued by Dousing Dragons (DD). Moriarty is trying to assess Cassidy's level of knowledge.

Moriarty asks Cassidy:

> "Why are clients willing to pay for structural and reduced form model analytics when they can get credit ratings for free?"

Cassidy identifies the following limitations of credit ratings:

Limitation A	The issuer-pays model may distort the accuracy of credit ratings.
Limitation B	Credit ratings tend to vary across time and across the business cycle.
Limitation C	Credit ratings do not provide an estimate of a bond's default probability.

Cassidy is asked to consider the use of a structural model of credit risk to analyze DD's bonds. Cassidy knows that holding DD's equity is economically equivalent to owning a type of security that is linked to DD's assets. However, Cassidy cannot remember the type of security or why this is true. Moriarty provides a hint:

> "It is true because equity shareholders have limited liability."

Moriarty asks Cassidy to analyze one of DD's bonds using data presented in Exhibit 1 and a reduced form model.

EXHIBIT 1 Dousing Dragons, Inc. Credit Analysis Worksheet

Coupon rate:	0.875%	**Coupon Payments:**	Semiannual
Face value:	1,000		
Today's date:	August 15, 2014	**Maturity date:**	August 15, 2018

Payment dates:	Risk-Free Zero Coupon Yields (%)	Credit Spread (%)	Total Yield (%)	Years to Maturity	Discount Factor	Cash Flow	Present Value	Risk-Free Discount Factor	Risk-Free Present Value
2/15/2015	0.13	0.12	0.25	0.50	0.99880	4.38	4.3747	0.9994	4.3774
8/15/2015	0.20	0.24	0.44	1.00	0.99560	4.38	4.3607	0.9980	4.3712
2/15/2016	0.23	0.31	0.54	1.50	0.99200	4.38	4.3450	0.9966	4.3651
8/15/2016	0.28	0.37	0.65	2.00	0.98710	4.38	4.3235	0.9944	4.3555
2/15/2017	0.32	0.38	0.70	2.50	0.98270	4.38	4.3042	0.9920	4.3450
8/15/2017	0.35	0.39	0.74	3.00	0.97810	4.38	4.2841	0.9896	4.3344
2/15/2018	0.44	0.43	0.87	3.50	0.97010	4.38	4.2490	0.9848	4.3134
8/15/2018	0.47	0.46	0.93	4.00	0.96370	1,004.38	967.9210	0.9814	985.6985
Total value:							998.1623		1,016.1606

Moriarty also asks Cassidy to discuss the similarities and differences in the analysis of asset-backed securities (ABS) and corporate debt. Cassidy states that:

Statement 1. Credit analysis for ABS and corporate bonds incorporates the same credit measures: probability of default, expected loss, and present value of expected loss.

Statement 2. Credit analysis for ABS and corporate bonds is different due to their future cash flow structures.

Statement 3. Credit analysis for ABS and corporate bonds can be done using either a structural or a reduced form model.

1. Which of Cassidy's stated limitations of credit ratings is *incorrect*?
   A. Limitation A
   B. Limitation B
   C. Limitation C
2. Given Moriarty's hint, Cassidy should *most likely* identify the type of security as a European:
   A. put option.
   B. call option.
   C. debt option.
3. The model chosen by Moriarty to analyze one of DD's bonds requires that:
   A. the equity of DD is traded.
   B. the assets of DD are traded.
   C. some of the debt of DD is traded.
4. Compared to a structural model, which of the following estimation approaches will Moriarty's choice of credit model allow him to use?
   A. Implicit
   B. Historical
   C. Calibration
5. Compared to a structural model, an advantage of the model chosen by Moriarty to analyze DD's bond is *most likely* that:
   A. its measures reflect the changing business cycle.
   B. it requires a specification of the company's balance sheet.
   C. it is possible to estimate the expected present value of expected loss.
6. Based on Exhibit 1, the present value of the expected loss due to credit risk on the bond is *closest* to:
   A. 1.84.
   B. 16.16.
   C. 18.00.
7. Based on Exhibit 1, the present value of the expected loss due to credit risk relating to the single promised payment scheduled on February 15, 2017, is *closest* to:
   A. 0.04.
   B. 0.08.
   C. 0.11.
8. Which of Cassidy's statements relating to the similarities and differences between the credit analysis of ABS and corporate bonds is *incorrect*?
   A. Statement 1
   B. Statement 2
   C. Statement 3

CHAPTER 7

INTRODUCTION TO ASSET-BACKED SECURITIES

LEARNING OUTCOMES

After completing this chapter, you will be able to do the following:

- explain benefits of securitization for economies and financial markets;
- describe the securitization process, including the parties to the process, the roles they play, and the legal structures involved;
- describe types and characteristics of residential mortgage loans that are typically securitized;
- describe types and characteristics of residential mortgage-backed securities, and explain the cash flows and credit risk for each type;
- explain the motivation for creating securitized structures with multiple tranches (e.g., collateralized mortgage obligations), and the characteristics and risks of securitized structures;
- describe the characteristics and risks of commercial mortgage-backed securities;
- describe types and characteristics of non-mortgage asset-backed securities, including the cash flows and credit risk of each type;
- describe collateralized debt obligations, including their cash flows and credit risk.

SUMMARY OVERVIEW

- The securitization process involves pooling relatively straight-forward debt obligations, such as loans or bonds, and using the cash flows from the pool of debt obligations to pay off the bond created in the securitization process.
- Securitization has several benefits. It allows investors direct access to liquid investments and payment streams that would be unattainable if all the financing were performed through banks. It enables banks to increase loan origination, monitoring, and collections at economic scales greater than if they used only their own in-house loan portfolios. The end result is lower costs of borrowing for entities raising funds, higher risk-adjusted returns to investors, and greater efficiency and profitability for the banking sector.

- The parties to a securitization include the special purpose vehicle (SPV, also called the trust) that is the issuer of the securities and the seller of the pool of loans (also called the depositor). The SPV is a bankruptcy-remote vehicle that plays a pivotal role in the securitization process.
- The securities issued are called asset-backed securities (ABS) or mortgage-backed securities (MBS) when the assets that are securitized are mortgage loans. A common structure in a securitization is subordination, which leads to the creation of more than one bond class or tranche. Bond classes differ as to how they will share any losses resulting from defaults of the borrowers whose loans are in the collateral (pool of loans). The credit ratings assigned to the various bond classes depends on how the credit-rating agencies evaluate the credit risks of the collateral and any credit enhancements.
- The payments that are received from the collateral are distributed to pay interest and repay principal to the security holders as well as to pay servicing and other fees. The details regarding the priority of payments are set forth in the structure's waterfall.
- The motivation for the creation of different types of structures is to redistribute prepayment risk and credit risk efficiently among different bond classes in the securitization. Prepayment risk is the uncertainty that the actual cash flows will be different from the scheduled cash flows as set forth in the loan agreements because borrowers may alter payments to take advantage of interest rate movements.
- Because of the SPV, the securitization of a company's assets may include some bond classes that have better credit ratings than the company itself or its corporate bonds. Thus, in the aggregate, the company's funding cost is often lower when raising funds through securitization than by issuing corporate bonds.
- A mortgage loan is a loan secured by the collateral of some specified real estate property which obliges the borrower to make a predetermined series of payments to the lender. The cash flow of a mortgage includes (1) interest, (2) scheduled principal payments, and (3) prepayments (any principal repaid in excess of the scheduled principal). The ratio of the property's purchase price to the amount of the mortgage is called the loan-to-value ratio.
- The various mortgage designs throughout the world specify (1) the maturity of the loan, (2) how the interest rate is determined (i.e., fixed rate versus adjustable or variable rate), (3) how the principal is repaid (i.e., whether the loan is amortizing or not and if it is, whether it is fully amortizing or partially amortizing with a balloon payment), (4) whether the borrower has the option to prepay and in this case, whether any prepayment penalties might be imposed, and (5) the rights of the lender in a foreclosure (i.e., whether the loan is a recourse or non-recourse loan).
- In the United States, there are three sectors for securities backed by residential mortgages: (1) those guaranteed by a federal agency (Ginnie Mae) whose securities are backed by the full faith and credit of the US government, (2) those guaranteed by either of the two GSEs (Fannie Mae and Freddie Mac) but not by the US government, and (3) those issued by private entities that are not guaranteed by a federal agency or a GSE. The first two sectors are referred to as agency residential mortgage-backed securities (RMBS), and the third sector as non-agency RMBS.
- A mortgage pass-through security is created when one or more holders of mortgages form a pool of mortgages and sell shares or participation certificates in the pool. The cash flow of a mortgage pass-through security depends on the cash flow of the underlying pool of mortgages and consists of monthly mortgage payments representing interest, the scheduled repayment of principal, and any prepayments, net of servicing and other fees.
- Market participants measure the prepayment rate using two measures: the single monthly mortality (SMM) rate and its corresponding annualized rate, namely, the conditional

prepayment rate (CPR). For MBS, the measure widely used by market participants to assess the sensitivity of the securitized bonds to interest rate movements is the weighted average life (WAL) or simply average life of the MBS instead of duration.

- Market participants use the Public Securities Association (PSA) prepayment benchmark to describe prepayment rates. A PSA assumption greater than 100 PSA means that prepayments are assumed to be faster than the benchmark, whereas a PSA assumption lower than 100 PSA means that prepayments are assumed to be slower than the benchmark.
- Prepayment risk includes two components: contraction risk and extension risk. The former is the risk that when interest rates decline, the security will have a shorter maturity than was anticipated at the time of purchase because homeowners refinance at now-available lower interest rates. The latter is the risk that when interest rates rise, fewer prepayments will occur because homeowners are reluctant to give up the benefits of a contractual interest rate that now looks low.
- The creation of a collateralized mortgage obligation (CMO) can help manage prepayment risk by distributing the various forms of prepayment risk among different classes of bondholders. The CMO's major financial innovation is that the securities created more closely satisfy the asset/liability needs of institutional investors, thereby broadening the appeal of mortgage-backed products.
- The most common types of CMO tranches are sequential-pay tranches, planned amortization class (PAC) tranches, support tranches, and floating-rate tranches.
- Non-agency RMBS share many features and structuring techniques with agency CMOs. However, they typically include two complementary mechanisms. First, the cash flows are distributed by rules, such as the waterfall, that dictate the allocation of interest payments and principal repayments to tranches with various degrees of priority/seniority. Second, there are rules for the allocation of realized losses, which specify that subordinated bond classes have lower payment priority than senior classes.
- In order to obtain favorable credit rating, non-agency RMBS and non-mortgage ABS often require one or more credit enhancements. The most common forms of internal credit enhancement are senior/subordinated structures, reserve funds, and overcollateralization. In external credit enhancement, credit support in the case of defaults resulting in losses in the pool of loans is provided in the form of a financial guarantee by a third party to the transaction.
- Commercial mortgage-backed securities (CMBS) are securities backed by a pool of commercial mortgage loans on income-producing property.
- Two key indicators of the potential credit performance of CMBS are the debt-to-service-coverage ratio and the loan-to-value ratio. The DSC ratio is the property's annual net operating income divided by the debt service.
- CMBS have considerable call protection, which allows CMBS to trade in the market more like corporate bonds than like RMBS. This call protection comes in two forms: at the structure level and at the loan level. The creation of sequential-pay tranches is an example of call protection at the structure level. At the loan level, four mechanisms offer investors call protection: prepayment lockouts, prepayment penalty points, yield maintenance charges, and defeasance.
- ABS are backed by a wide range of asset types. The most popular non-mortgage ABS are auto loan receivable-backed securities and credit card receivable-backed securities. The collateral is amortizing for auto loan-backed securities and non-amortizing for credit card receivable-backed securities. As with non-agency RMBS, these ABS must offer credit enhancement to be appealing to investors.

- A collateralized debt obligation (CDO) is a generic term used to describe a security backed by a diversified pool of one or more debt obligations (e.g., corporate and emerging market bonds, leveraged bank loans, ABS, RMBS, CMBS, or CDO).
- Like an ABS, a CDO involves the creation of an SPV. But in contrary to an ABS where the funds necessary to pay the bond classes come from a pool of loans that must be serviced, a CDO requires a collateral manager to buy and sell debt obligations for and from the CDO's portfolio of assets to generate sufficient cash flows to meet the obligations of the CDO bondholders and to generate a fair return for the equity holders.
- The structure of a CDO includes senior, mezzanine, and subordinated/equity bond classes.

PROBLEMS

1. Securitization is beneficial for banks because it:
   A. repackages bank loans into simpler structures.
   B. increases the funds available for banks to lend.
   C. allows banks to maintain ownership of their securitized assets.
2. In a securitization, a special purpose vehicle (SPV) is responsible for the:
   A. issuance of the asset-backed securities.
   B. collection of payments from the borrowers.
   C. recovery of underlying assets for delinquent loans.
3. In a securitization structure, time tranching provides investors with the ability to choose between:
   A. extension risk and contraction risk.
   B. fully amortizing loans and partially amortizing loans.
   C. senior bonds and subordinate bonds.
4. William Marolf obtains a 5 million EUR mortgage loan from Bank Nederlandse. A year later the principal on the loan is 4 million EUR and Marolf defaults on the loan. Bank Nederlandse forecloses, sells the property for 2.5 million EUR, and is entitled to collect the shortfall, 1.5 million EUR, from Marolf. Marolf *most likely* had a:
   A. bullet loan.
   B. recourse loan.
   C. non-recourse loan.
5. Fran Martin obtains a non-recourse mortgage loan for $500,000. One year later, when the outstanding balance of the mortgage is $490,000, Martin cannot make his mortgage payments and defaults on the loan. The lender forecloses on the loan and sells the house for $315,000. What amount is the lender entitled to claim from Martin?
   A. $0.
   B. $175,000.
   C. $185,000.
6. Anne Bogaert reviews the status of her home mortgage schedule for the month of January 2014:

Date	Item	Balance
01 January 2014	Outstanding mortgage loan balance	$500,000
31 January 2014	Total monthly required payment	$10,000
31 January 2014	Interest component of total monthly required payment	$2,500

On 31 January 2014, Boagert makes a payment of $15,000 rather than $10,000. What will be the outstanding mortgage loan balance immediately after the payment is made?

A. $485,000
B. $487,500
C. $490,000

7. Which of the following describes a typical feature of a non-agency residential mortgage-backed security (RMBS)?
   A. Senior-subordinate structure in bond classes
   B. A pool of conforming mortgages as collateral
   C. A guarantee by the appropriate government sponsored enterprise (GSE)
8. Maria Nyugen is an analyst for an insurance company that invests in residential mortgage pass-through securities. Nyugen reviews the monthly cash flow of one underlying mortgage pool to determine the cash flow to be passed through to investors:

Total principal paid including prepayment	$1,910,542
Scheduled principal to be paid before prepayment	$910,542
Gross coupon interest paid	$3,562,500
Servicing fees	$337,500
Other fees for guaranteeing the issue	$58,333

Based on Nyugen's table, the total cash flow to be passed through to the investors is *closest* to:

A. $4,473,042.
B. $5,077,209.
C. $5,473,042.

9. In the context of mortgage-backed securities, a conditional prepayment rate (CPR) of 8% means that approximately 8% of an outstanding mortgage pool balance at the beginning of the year will be prepaid:
   A. in the current month.
   B. by the end of the year.
   C. over the life of the mortgages.
10. For a mortgage pass-through security, which of the following risks *most likely* increases as interest rates decline?
    A. Balloon
    B. Extension
    C. Contraction
11. From a lender's perspective, balloon risk can *best* be described as a type of:
    A. extension risk.
    B. contraction risk.
    C. interest rate risk.
12. Credit risk is a factor for commercial mortgage-backed securities because they are backed by mortgage loans that:
    A. are non-recourse.
    B. have limited call protection.
    C. have no prepayment penalty points.

13. Which commercial mortgage-backed security (CMBS) characteristic causes CMBS to trade more like a corporate bond than an agency residential mortgage-backed security (RMBS)?
    A. Call protection
    B. Internal credit enhancement
    C. Debt-to-service coverage ratio level
14. An excess spread account incorporated into a securitized structure is designed to limit:
    A. credit risk.
    B. extension risk.
    C. contraction risk.
15. Which of the following *best* describes the cash flow that owners of credit card receivable-backed securities receive during the lockout period?
    A. Only principal payments collected
    B. Only finance charges and fees collected
    C. No cash flow is received as all cash flow collected is reinvested.

CHAPTER 8

THE ARBITRAGE-FREE VALUATION FRAMEWORK

LEARNING OUTCOMES

After completing this chapter, you will be able to do the following:

- explain what is meant by arbitrage-free valuation of a fixed-income instrument;
- calculate the arbitrage-free value of an option-free, fixed-rate coupon bond;
- describe a binomial interest rate tree framework;
- describe the backward induction valuation methodology and calculate the value of a fixed-income instrument given its cash flow at each node;
- describe the process of calibrating a binomial interest rate tree to match a specific term structure;
- compare pricing using the zero-coupon yield curve with pricing using an arbitrage-free binomial lattice;
- describe pathwise valuation in a binomial interest rate framework and calculate the value of a fixed-income instrument given its cash flows along each path;
- describe a Monte Carlo forward-rate simulation and its application.

SUMMARY OVERVIEW

This chapter presents the principles and tools for arbitrage valuation of fixed-income securities. Much of the discussion centers on the binomial interest rate tree, which can be used extensively to value both option-free bonds and bonds with embedded options. The following are the main points made in the chapter:

- A fundamental principle of valuation is that the value of any financial asset is equal to the present value of its expected future cash flows.
- A fixed-income security is a portfolio of zero-coupon bonds.
- Each zero-coupon bond has its own discount rate that depends on the shape of the yield curve and when the cash flow is delivered in time.

- In well-functioning markets, prices adjust until there are no opportunities for arbitrage.
- The law of one price states that two goods that are perfect substitutes must sell for the same current price in the absence of transaction costs.
- An arbitrage opportunity is a transaction that involves no cash outlay yet results in a riskless profit.
- Using the arbitrage-free approach, viewing a security as a package of zero-coupon bonds means that two bonds with the same maturity and different coupon rates are viewed as different packages of zero-coupon bonds and valued accordingly.
- For bonds that are option free, an arbitrage-free value is simply the present value of expected future values using the benchmark spot rates.
- A binomial interest rate tree permits the short interest rate to take on one of two possible values consistent with the volatility assumption and an interest rate model.
- An interest rate tree is a visual representation of the possible values of interest rates (forward rates) based on an interest rate model and an assumption about interest rate volatility.
- The possible interest rates for any following period are consistent with the following three assumptions: (1) an interest rate model that governs the random process of interest rates, (2) the assumed level of interest rate volatility, and (3) the current benchmark yield curve.
- From the lognormal distribution, adjacent interest rates on the tree are multiples of e raised to the 2σ power.
- One of the benefits of a lognormal distribution is that if interest rates get too close to zero, then the absolute change in interest rates becomes smaller and smaller.
- We use the backward induction valuation methodology that involves starting at maturity, filling in those values, and working back from right to left to find the bond's value at the desired node.
- The interest rate tree is fit to the current yield curve by choosing interest rates that result in the benchmark bond value. By doing this, the bond value is arbitrage free.
- An option-free bond that is valued by using the binomial interest rate tree should have the same value as discounting by the spot rates.
- Pathwise valuation calculates the present value of a bond for each possible interest rate path and takes the average of these values across paths.
- The Monte Carlo method is an alternative method for simulating a sufficiently large number of potential interest rate paths in an effort to discover how the value of a security is affected and involves randomly selecting paths in an effort to approximate the results of a complete pathwise valuation.

PROBLEMS

This item set was developed by Karen O'Connor Rubsam, CFA (Phoenix, AZ, USA). Copyright © 2014 CFA Institute.

The following information relates to Questions 1–6

Katrina Black, portfolio manager at Coral Bond Management, Ltd., is conducting a training session with Alex Sun, a junior analyst in the fixed income department. Black wants to explain to Sun the arbitrage-free valuation framework used by the firm. Black presents Sun with Exhibit 1, showing a fictitious bond being traded on three exchanges, and asks Sun to identify the arbitrage opportunity of the bond. Sun agrees to ignore transaction costs in his analysis.

EXHIBIT 1 Three-Year, €100 par, 3.00% Coupon, Annual Pay Option-Free Bond

	Eurex	NYSE Euronext	Frankfurt
Price	€103.7956	€103.7815	€103.7565

Black shows Sun some exhibits that were part of a recent presentation. Exhibit 3 presents most of the data of a binomial lognormal interest rate tree fit to the yield curve shown in Exhibit 2. Exhibit 4 presents most of the data of the implied values for a four-year, option-free, annual pay bond with a 2.5% coupon based on the information in Exhibit 3.

EXHIBIT 2 Yield to Maturity Par Rates for One-, Two-, and Three-Year Annual Pay Option-Free Bonds

One-Year	Two-Year	Three-Year
1.25%	1.50%	1.70%

EXHIBIT 3 Binomial Interest Rate Tree Fit to the Yield Curve (Volatility = 10%)

Current	Year 1	Year 2	Year 3	Year 4
1.2500%	1.8229%	1.8280%	2.6241%	**Node 4–1**
	1.4925%	**Node 2–2**	**Node 3–2**	4.2009%
		1.2254%	1.7590%	3.4394%
			Node 3–4	2.8159%
				Node 4–5

EXHIBIT 4 Implied Values (in Euros) for a 2.5%, Four-Year, Option-Free, Annual Pay Bond Based on Exhibit 3

Year 0	Year 1	Year 2	Year 3	Year 4
103.4960	104.2876	103.2695	102.3791	102.5000
	Node 1–2	104.0168	102.8442	102.5000
		104.6350	103.2282	102.5000
			103.5448	102.5000
				102.5000

Black asks about the missing data in Exhibits 3 and 4 and directs Sun to complete the following tasks related to those exhibits:

Task 1 Test that the binomial interest tree has been properly calibrated to be arbitrage-free.

Task 2 Develop a spreadsheet model to calculate pathwise valuations. To test the accuracy of the spreadsheet, use the data in Exhibit 3 and calculate the value of the bond if it takes a path of lowest rates in Year 1 and Year 2 and the second lowest rate in Year 3.

Task 3	Identify a type of bond where the Monte Carlo calibration method should be used in place of the binomial interest rate method.
Task 4	Update Exhibit 3 to reflect the current volatility, which is now 15%.

1. Based on Exhibit 1, the *best* action that an investor should take to profit from the arbitrage opportunity is to:
   A. buy on Frankfurt, sell on Eurex.
   B. buy on NYSE Euronext, sell on Eurex.
   C. buy on Frankfurt, sell on NYSE Euronext.
2. Based on Exhibits 1 and 2, the exchange that reflects the arbitrage-free price of the bond is:
   A. Eurex.
   B. Frankfurt.
   C. NYSE Euronext.
3. Which of the following statements about the missing data in Exhibit 3 is correct?
   A. Node 3–2 can be derived from Node 2–2.
   B. Node 4–1 should be equal to Node 4–5 multiplied by $e^{0.4}$.
   C. Node 2–2 approximates the implied one-year forward rate one year from now.
4. Based on the information in Exhibits 3 and 4, the bond price in euros at Node 1–2 in Exhibit 4 is *closest* to:
   A. 102.7917.
   B. 104.8640.
   C. 105.2917.
5. A benefit of performing Task 1 is that it:
   A. enables the model to price bonds with embedded options.
   B. identifies benchmark bonds that have been mispriced by the market.
   C. allows investors to realize arbitrage profits through stripping and reconstitution.
6. If the assumed volatility is changed as Black requested in Task 4, the forward rates shown in Exhibit 3 will *most likely*:
   A. spread out.
   B. remain unchanged.
   C. converge to the spot rates.

The following information relates to Questions 7–10[1]

Betty Tatton is a fixed income analyst with the hedge fund Sailboat Asset Management (SAM). SAM invests in a variety of global fixed-income strategies, including fixed-income arbitrage. Tatton is responsible for pricing individual investments and analyzing market data to assess the opportunity for arbitrage. She uses two methods to value bonds:

Method 1	Discount each year's cash flow separately using the appropriate interest rate curve.
Method 2	Build and use a binomial interest rate tree.

[1] This question set was developed by Jennie I. Sanders, CFA (Brooklyn, NY, USA).

Tatton compiles pricing data for a list of annual pay bonds (Exhibit 1). Each of the bonds will mature in two years, and Tatton considers the bonds as being risk-free; both the one-year and two-year benchmark spot rates are 2%. Tatton calculates the arbitrage-free prices and identifies an arbitrage opportunity to recommend to her team.

EXHIBIT 1 Market Data for Selected Bonds

Asset	Coupon	Market Price
Bond A	1%	98.0584
Bond B	3%	100.9641
Bond C	5%	105.8247

Next, Tatton uses the benchmark yield curve provided in Exhibit 2 to consider arbitrage opportunities of both option-free corporate bonds and corporate bonds with embedded options. The benchmark bonds in Exhibit 2 pay coupons annually, and the bonds are priced at par.

EXHIBIT 2 Benchmark Par Curve

Maturity (years)	Yield to Maturity (YTM)
1	3.0%
2	4.0%
3	5.0%

Tatton then identifies three mispriced three-year annual-pay bonds and compiles data on the bonds (see Exhibit 3).

EXHIBIT 3 Market Data of Annual-Pay Corporate Bonds

Company	Coupon	Market Price	Yield	Embedded Option?
Hutto-Barkley Inc.	3%	94.9984	5.6%	No
Luna y Estrellas Intl.	0%	88.8996	4.0%	Yes
Peaton Scorpio Motors	0%	83.9619	6.0%	No

Lastly, Tatton identifies two mispriced Swiss bonds, Bond X, a three-year bond, and Bond Y, a five-year bond. Both are annual-pay bonds with a coupon rate of 6%. To calculate the bonds' values, Tatton devises the first three years of the interest rate lognormal tree presented in Exhibit 4 using historical interest rate volatility data. Tatton considers how this data would change if implied volatility, which is higher than historical volatility, were used instead.

EXHIBIT 4 Interest Rate Tree; Forward Rates Based on Swiss Market

Year 1	Year 2	Year 3
	4%	6%
1%		5%
	2%	3%

7. Based on Exhibit 1, which of the following bonds *most likely* includes an arbitrage opportunity?
   A. Bond A
   B. Bond B
   C. Bond C
8. Based on Exhibits 2 and 3 and using Method 1, the amount (in absolute terms) by which the Hutto-Barkley corporate bond is mispriced is *closest* to:
   A. 0.3368 per 100 of par value.
   B. 0.4682 per 100 of par value.
   C. 0.5156 per 100 of par value.
9. Method 1 would *most likely* **not** be an appropriate valuation technique for the bond issued by:
   A. Hutto-Barkley Inc.
   B. Luna y Estrellas Intl.
   C. Peaton Scorpio Motors.
10. Based on Exhibit 4 and using Method 2, the correct price for Bond X is *closest* to:
    A. 97.2998.
    B. 109.0085.
    C. 115.0085.

CHAPTER 9

VALUATION AND ANALYSIS: BONDS WITH EMBEDDED OPTIONS

LEARNING OUTCOMES

After completing this chapter, you will be able to do the following:

- describe fixed-income securities with embedded options;
- explain the relationships between the values of a callable or putable bond, the underlying option-free (straight) bond, and the embedded option;
- describe how the arbitrage-free framework can be used to value a bond with embedded options;
- explain how interest rate volatility affects the value of a callable or putable bond;
- explain how changes in the level and shape of the yield curve affect the value of a callable or putable bond;
- calculate the value of a callable or putable bond from an interest rate tree;
- explain the calculation and use of option-adjusted spreads;
- explain how interest rate volatility affects option-adjusted spreads;
- calculate and interpret effective duration of a callable or putable bond;
- compare effective durations of callable, putable, and straight bonds;
- describe the use of one-sided durations and key rate durations to evaluate the interest rate sensitivity of bonds with embedded options;
- compare effective convexities of callable, putable, and straight bonds;
- calculate the value of a capped or floored floating-rate bond;
- describe defining features of a convertible bond;
- calculate and interpret the components of a convertible bond's value;
- describe how a convertible bond is valued in an arbitrage-free framework;
- compare the risk–return characteristics of a convertible bond with the risk–return characteristics of a straight bond and of the underlying common stock.

SUMMARY OVERVIEW

This chapter covers the valuation and analysis of bonds with embedded options. The following are the main points made in this chapter:

- An embedded option represents a right that can be exercised by the issuer, by the bondholder, or automatically depending on the course of interest rates. It is attached to, or embedded in, an underlying option-free bond called a straight bond.
- Simple embedded option structures include call options, put options, and extension options. Callable and putable bonds can be redeemed prior to maturity, at the discretion of the issuer in the former case and of the bondholder in the latter case. An extendible bond gives the bondholder the right to keep the bond for a number of years after maturity. Putable and extendible bonds are equivalent, except that the underlying option-free bonds are different.
- Complex embedded option structures include bonds with other types of options or combinations of options. For example, a convertible bond includes a conversion option that allows the bondholders to convert their bonds into the issuer's common stock. A bond with an estate put can be put by the heirs of a deceased bondholder. Sinking fund bonds make the issuer set aside funds over time to retire the bond issue and are often callable, may have an acceleration provision, and may also contain a delivery option. Valuing and analyzing bonds with complex embedded option structures is challenging.
- According to the arbitrage-free framework, the value of a bond with an embedded option is equal to the arbitrage-free values of its parts—that is, the arbitrage-free value of the straight bond and the arbitrage-free values of each of the embedded options.
- Because the call option is an issuer option, the value of the call option decreases the value of the callable bond relative to an otherwise identical but non-callable bond. In contrast, because the put option is an investor option, the value of the put option increases the value of the putable bond relative to an otherwise identical but non-putable bond.
- In the absence of default and interest rate volatility, the bond's future cash flows are certain. Thus, the value of a callable or putable bond can be calculated by discounting the bond's future cash flows at the appropriate one-period forward rates, taking into consideration the decision to exercise the option. If a bond is callable, the decision to exercise the option is made by the issuer, which will exercise the call option when the value of the bond's future cash flows is higher than the call price. In contrast, if the bond is putable, the decision to exercise the option is made by the bondholder, who will exercise the put option when the value of the bond's future cash flows is lower than the put price.
- In practice, interest rates fluctuate, and interest rate volatility affects the value of embedded options. Thus, when valuing bonds with embedded options, it is important to consider the possible evolution of the yield curve over time.
- Interest rate volatility is modeled using a binomial interest rate tree. The higher the volatility, the lower the value of the callable bond and the higher the value of the putable bond.
- Valuing a bond with embedded options assuming an interest rate volatility requires three steps: (1) Generate a tree of interest rates based on the given yield curve and volatility assumptions; (2) at each node of the tree, determine whether the embedded options will be exercised; and (3) apply the backward induction valuation methodology to calculate the present value of the bond.
- The most commonly used approach to valuing risky bonds is to add a spread to the one-period forward rates used to discount the bond's future cash flows.

- The option-adjusted spread is the single spread added uniformly to the one-period forward rates on the tree to produce a value or price for a bond. OAS is sensitive to interest rate volatility: The higher the volatility, the lower the OAS for a callable bond.
- For bonds with embedded options, the best measure to assess the sensitivity of the bond's price to a parallel shift of the benchmark yield curve is effective duration. The effective duration of a callable or putable bond cannot exceed that of the straight bond.
- The effective convexity of a straight bond is negligible, but that of bonds with embedded options is not. When the option is near the money, the convexity of a callable bond is negative, indicating that the upside for a callable bond is much smaller than the downside, whereas the convexity of a putable bond is positive, indicating that the upside for a putable bond is much larger than the downside.
- Because the prices of callable and putable bonds respond asymmetrically to upward and downward interest rate changes of the same magnitude, one-sided durations provide a better indication regarding the interest rate sensitivity of bonds with embedded options than (two-sided) effective duration.
- Key rate durations show the effect of shifting only key points, one at a time, rather than the entire yield curve.
- The arbitrage-free framework can be used to value capped and floored floaters. The cap provision in a floater is an issuer option that prevents the coupon rate from increasing above a specified maximum rate. Thus, the value of a capped floater is equal to or less than the value of the straight bond. In contrast, the floor provision in a floater is an investor option that prevents the coupon from decreasing below a specified minimum rate. Thus, the value of a floored floater is equal to or higher than the value of the straight bond.
- The characteristics of a convertible bond include the conversion price, which is the applicable share price at which the bondholders can convert their bonds into common shares, and the conversion ratio, which reflects the number of shares of common stock that the bondholders receive from converting their bonds into shares. The conversion price is adjusted in case of corporate actions, such as stock splits, bonus share issuances, and rights and warrants issuances. Convertible bondholders may receive compensation when the issuer pays dividends to its common shareholders, and they may be given the opportunity to either put their bonds or convert their bonds into shares earlier and at more advantageous terms in the case of a change of control.
- There are a number of investment metrics and ratios that help analyze and value convertible bonds. The conversion value indicates the value of the bond if it is converted at the market price of the shares. The minimum value of a convertible bond sets a floor value for the convertible bond at the greater of the conversion value or the straight value. This floor is moving, however, because the straight value is not fixed. The market conversion premium represents the price investors effectively pay for the underlying shares if they buy the convertible bond and then convert it into shares. Scaled by the market price of the shares, it represents the premium payable when buying the convertible bond rather than the underlying common stock.
- Because convertible bonds combine characteristics of bonds, stocks, and options, as well as potentially other features, their valuation and analysis is challenging. Convertible bond investors should consider the factors that affect not only bond prices but also the underlying share price.
- The arbitrage-free framework can be used to value convertible bonds, including callable and putable ones. Each component (straight bond, call option of the stock, and call and/or put option on the bond) can be valued separately.

- The risk–return characteristics of a convertible bond depend on the underlying share price relative to the conversion price. When the underlying share price is well below the conversion price, the convertible bond is "busted" and exhibits mostly bond risk–return characteristics. Thus, it is mainly sensitive to interest rate movements. In contrast, when the underlying share price is well above the conversion price, the convertible bond exhibits mostly stock risk–return characteristics. Thus, its price follows similar movements to the price of the underlying stock. In between these two extremes, the convertible bond trades like a hybrid instrument.

PROBLEMS

The following information relates to Questions 1–10[1]

Samuel & Sons is a fixed-income specialty firm that offers advisory services to investment management companies. On 1 October 20X0, Steele Ferguson, a senior analyst at Samuel, is reviewing three fixed-rate bonds issued by a local firm, Pro Star, Inc. The three bonds, whose characteristics are given in Exhibit 1, carry the highest credit rating.

EXHIBIT 1 Fixed-Rate Bonds Issued by Pro Star, Inc.

Bond	Maturity	Coupon	Type of Bond
Bond #1	1 October 20X3	4.40% annual	Option-free
Bond #2	1 October 20X3	4.40% annual	Callable at par on 1 October 20X1 and on 1 October 20X2
Bond #3	1 October 20X3	4.40% annual	Putable at par on 1 October 20X1 and on 1 October 20X2

The one-year, two-year, and three-year par rates are 2.250%, 2.750%, and 3.100%, respectively. Based on an estimated interest rate volatility of 10%, Ferguson constructs the binomial interest rate tree shown in Exhibit 2.

EXHIBIT 2 Binomial Interest Rate Tree

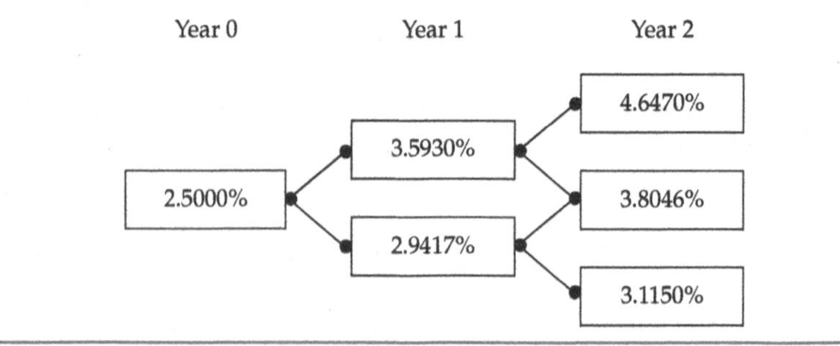

[1] This question set was developed by Danny Hassett, CFA (Arlington, TX, USA) and Ioannis Georgiou, CFA (Cyprus).

On 19 October 20X0, Ferguson analyzes the convertible bond issued by Pro Star given in Exhibit 3. That day, the market prices of Pro Star's convertible bond and common stock are $1,060 and $37.50, respectively.

EXHIBIT 3 Convertible Bond Issued by Pro Star, Inc.

Issue Date:	6 December 20X0
Maturity Date:	6 December 20X4
Coupon Rate:	2%
Issue Price:	$1,000
Conversion Ratio:	31

1. The call feature of Bond #2 is *best* described as:
   A. European style.
   B. American style.
   C. Bermudan style.
2. The bond that would *most likely* protect investors against a significant increase in interest rates is:
   A. Bond #1.
   B. Bond #2.
   C. Bond #3.
3. A fall in interest rates would *most likely* result in:
   A. a decrease in the effective duration of Bond #3.
   B. Bond #3 having more upside potential than Bond #2.
   C. a change in the effective convexity of Bond #3 from positive to negative.
4. The value of Bond #2 is *closest* to:
   A. 102.103% of par.
   B. 103.121% of par.
   C. 103.744% of par.
5. The value of Bond #3 is *closest* to:
   A. 102.103% of par.
   B. 103.688% of par.
   C. 103.744% of par.
6. All else being equal, a rise in interest rates will *most likely* result in the value of the option embedded in Bond #3:
   A. decreasing.
   B. remaining unchanged.
   C. increasing.
7. All else being equal, if Ferguson assumes an interest rate volatility of 15% instead of 10%, the bond that would *most likely* increase in value is:
   A. Bond #1.
   B. Bond #2.
   C. Bond #3.
8. All else being equal, if the shape of the yield curve changes from upward sloping to flattening, the value of the option embedded in Bond #2 will *most likely*:
   A. decrease.
   B. remain unchanged.
   C. increase.

9. The conversion price of the bond in Exhibit 3 is *closest* to:
   A. $26.67.
   B. $32.26.
   C. $34.19.
10. If the market price of Pro Star's common stock falls from its level on 19 October 20X0, the price of the convertible bond will *most likely*:
    A. fall at the same rate as Pro Star's stock price.
    B. fall but at a slightly lower rate than Pro Star's stock price.
    C. be unaffected until Pro Star's stock price reaches the conversion price.

The following information relates to Question 11–19[2]

Rayes Investment Advisers specializes in fixed-income portfolio management. Meg Rayes, the owner of the firm, would like to add bonds with embedded options to the firm's bond portfolio. Rayes has asked Mingfang Hsu, one of the firm's analysts, to assist her in selecting and analyzing bonds for possible inclusion in the firm's bond portfolio.

Hsu first selects two corporate bonds that are callable at par and have the same characteristics in terms of maturity, credit quality, and call dates. Hsu uses the option adjusted spread (OAS) approach to analyse the bonds, assuming an interest rate volatility of 10%. The results of his analysis are presented in Exhibit 1.

EXHIBIT 1 Summary Results of Hsu's Analysis Using the OAS Approach

Bond	OAS (in bps)
Bond #1	25.5
Bond #2	30.3

Hsu then selects the four bonds issued by RW, Inc. given in Exhibit 2. These bonds all have a maturity of three years and the same credit rating. Bonds #4 and #5 are identical to Bond #3, an option-free bond, except that they each include an embedded option.

EXHIBIT 2 Bonds Issued by RW, Inc.

Bond	Coupon	Special Provision
Bond #3	4.00% annual	
Bond #4	4.00% annual	Callable at par at the end of years 1 and 2
Bond #5	4.00% annual	Putable at par at the end of years 1 and 2
Bond #6	One-year Libor annually, set in arrears	

To value and analyze RW's bonds, Hsu uses an estimated interest rate volatility of 15% and constructs the binomial interest rate tree provided in Exhibit 3.

---

[2] This question set was developed by Dan Reeder, CFA (Shawnee, OK, USA) and Ioannis Georgiou, CFA (Cyprus).

EXHIBIT 3 Binomial Interest Rate Tree Used to Value RW's Bonds

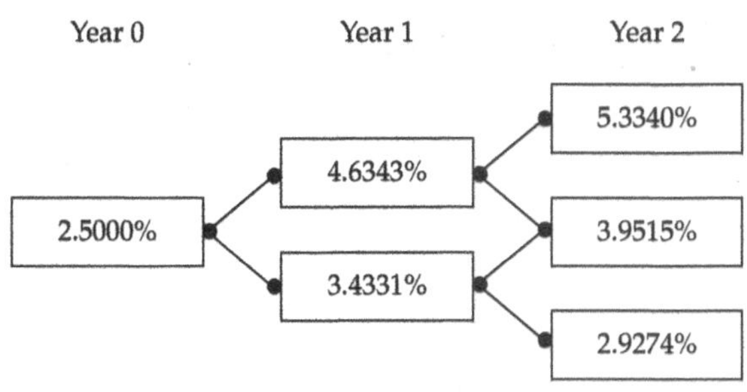

Rayes asks Hsu to determine the sensitivity of Bond #4's price to a 20 bps parallel shift of the benchmark yield curve. The results of Hsu's calculations are shown in Exhibit 4.

EXHIBIT 4 Summary Results of Hsu's Analysis about the Sensitivity of Bond #4's Price to a Parallel Shift of the Benchmark Yield Curve

Magnitude of the Parallel Shift in the Benchmark Yield Curve	+20 bps	–20 bps
Full Price of Bond #4 (% of par)	100.478	101.238

Hsu also selects the two floating-rate bonds issued by Varlep, plc given in Exhibit 5. These bonds have a maturity of three years and the same credit rating.

EXHIBIT 5 Floating-Rate Bonds Issued by Varlep, plc

Bond	Coupon
Bond #7	One-year Libor annually, set in arrears, capped at 5.00%
Bond #8	One-year Libor annually, set in arrears, floored at 3.50%

To value Varlep's bonds, Hsu constructs the binomial interest rate tree provided in Exhibit 6.

EXHIBIT 6 Binomial Interest Rate Tree Used to Value Varlep's Bonds

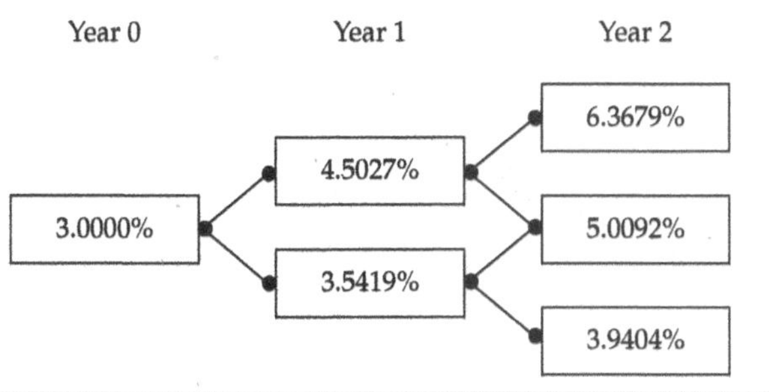

Last, Hsu selects the two bonds issued by Whorton, Inc. given in Exhibit 7. These bonds are close to their maturity date and are identical, except that Bond #9 includes a conversion option. Whorton's common stock is currently trading at $30 per share.

EXHIBIT 7 Bonds Issued by Whorton, Inc.

Bond	Type of Bond
Bond #9	Convertible bond with a conversion price of $50
Bond #10	Identical to Bond #9 except that it does not include a conversion option

11. Based on Exhibit 1, Rayes would *most likely* conclude that relative to Bond #1, Bond #2 is:
    A. overpriced.
    B. fairly priced.
    C. underpriced.
12. The effective duration of Bond #6 is:
    A. lower than or equal to 1.
    B. higher than 1 but lower than 3.
    C. higher than 3.
13. In Exhibit 2, the bond whose effective duration will lengthen if interest rates rise is:
    A. Bond #3.
    B. Bond #4.
    C. Bond #5.
14. The effective duration of Bond #4 is *closest* to:
    A. 0.76.
    B. 1.88.
    C. 3.77.
15. The value of Bond #7 is *closest* to:
    A. 99.697% of par.
    B. 99.936% of par.
    C. 101.153% of par.
16. The value of Bond #8 is *closest* to:
    A. 98.116% of par.
    B. 100.000% of par.
    C. 100.485% of par.
17. The value of Bond #9 is equal to the value of Bond #10:
    A. plus the value of a put option on Whorton's common stock.
    B. plus the value of a call option on Whorton's common stock.
    C. minus the value of a call option on Whorton's common stock.
18. The minimum value of Bond #9 is equal to the *greater* of:
    A. the conversion value of Bond #9 and the current value of Bond #10.
    B. the current value of Bond #10 and a call option on Whorton's common stock.
    C. the conversion value of Bond #9 and a call option on Whorton's common stock.
19. The factor that is currently *least likely* to affect the risk-return characteristics of Bond #9 is:
    A. Interest rate movements.
    B. Whorton's credit spreads.
    C. Whorton's common stock price movements.

CHAPTER 10

THE TERM STRUCTURE AND INTEREST RATE DYNAMICS

LEARNING OUTCOMES

After completing this chapter, you will be able to do the following:

- describe relationships among spot rates, forward rates, yield to maturity, expected and realized returns on bonds, and the shape of the yield curve;
- describe the forward pricing and forward rate models and calculate forward and spot prices and rates using those models;
- describe the assumptions concerning the evolution of spot rates in relation to forward rates implicit in active bond portfolio management;
- describe the strategy of riding the yield curve;
- explain the swap rate curve, and why and how market participants use it in valuation;
- calculate and interpret the swap spread for a default-free bond;
- describe the Z-spread;
- describe the TED and Libor–OIS spreads;
- explain traditional theories of the term structure of interest rates and describe the implications of each theory for forward rates and the shape of the yield curve;
- describe modern term structure models and how they are used;
- explain how a bond's exposure to each of the factors driving the yield curve can be measured and how these exposures can be used to manage yield curve risks;
- explain the maturity structure of yield volatilities and their effect on price volatility.

SUMMARY OVERVIEW

- The spot rate for a given maturity can be expressed as a geometric average of the short-term rate and a series of forward rates.
- Forward rates are above (below) spot rates when the spot curve is upward (downward) sloping, whereas forward rates are equal to spot rates when the spot curve is flat.

- If forward rates are realized, then all bonds, regardless of maturity, will have the same one-period realized return, which is the first-period spot rate.
- If the spot rate curve is upward sloping and is unchanged, then each bond "rolls down" the curve and earns the forward rate that rolls out of its pricing (i.e., a T^*-period zero-coupon bond earns the T^*-period forward rate as it rolls down to be a $T^* - 1$ period security). This implies an expected return in excess of short-maturity bonds (i.e., a term premium) for longer-maturity bonds if the yield curve is upward sloping.
- Active bond portfolio management is consistent with the expectation that today's forward curve does not accurately reflect future spot rates.
- The swap curve provides another measure of the time value of money.
- The swap markets are significant internationally because swaps are frequently used to hedge interest rate risk exposure.
- The swap spread, the I-spread, and the Z-spread are bond quoting conventions that can be used to determine a bond's price.
- Swap curves and Treasury curves can differ because of differences in their credit exposures, liquidity, and other supply/demand factors.
- The local expectations theory, liquidity preference theory, segmented markets theory, and preferred habitat theory provide traditional explanations for the shape of the yield curve.
- Modern finance seeks to provide models for the shape of the yield curve and the use of the yield curve to value bonds (including those with embedded options) and bond-related derivatives. General equilibrium and arbitrage-free models are the two major types of such models.
- Arbitrage-free models are frequently used to value bonds with embedded options. Unlike equilibrium models, arbitrage-free models begin with the observed market prices of a reference set of financial instruments, and the underlying assumption is that the reference set is correctly priced.
- Historical yield curve movements suggest that they can be explained by a linear combination of three principal movements: level, steepness, and curvature.
- The volatility term structure can be measured using historical data and depicts yield curve risk.
- The sensitivity of a bond value to yield curve changes may make use of effective duration, key rate durations, or sensitivities to parallel, steepness, and curvature movements. Using key rate durations or sensitivities to parallel, steepness, and curvature movements allows one to measure and manage shaping risk.

PROBLEMS

Prepared by Professor Adam Schwartz, CFA. Copyright © 2014 CFA Institute.

1. Given spot rates for one-, two-, and three-year zero coupon bonds, how many forward rates can be calculated?
2. Give two interpretations for the following forward rate: The two-year forward rate one year from now is 2%.
3. Describe the relationship between forward rates and spot rates if the yield curve is flat.
4. A. Define the yield to maturity for a coupon bond.
   B. Is it possible for a coupon bond to earn less than the yield to maturity if held to maturity?

5. If a bond trader believes that current forward rates overstate future spot rates, how might he or she profit from that conclusion?
6. Explain the strategy of riding the yield curve.
7. What are the advantages of using the swap curve as a benchmark of interest rates relative to a government bond yield curve?
8. Describe how the Z-spread can be used to price a bond.
9. What is the TED spread and what type of risk does it measure?
10. According to the local expectations theory, what would be the difference in the one-month total return if an investor purchased a five-year zero-coupon bond versus a two-year zero-coupon bond?
11. Compare the segmented market and the preferred habitat term structure theories.
12. A. List the three factors that have empirically been observed to affect Treasury security returns and explain how each of these factors affects returns on Treasury securities.
    B. What has been observed to be the most important factor in affecting Treasury returns?
    C. Which measures of yield curve risk can measure shaping risk?
13. Which forward rate cannot be computed from the one-, two-, three-, and four-year spot rates? The rate for a:
    A. one-year loan beginning in two years.
    B. two-year loan beginning in two years.
    C. three-year loan beginning in two years.
14. Consider spot rates for three zero-coupon bonds: $r(1) = 3\%$, $r(2) = 4\%$, and $r(3) = 5\%$. Which statement is correct? The forward rate for a one-year loan beginning in one year will be:
    A. less than the forward rate for a one-year loan beginning in two-years.
    B. greater than the forward rate for a two-year loan beginning in one-year.
    C. greater than the forward rate for a one-year loan beginning in two-years.
15. If one-period forward rates are decreasing with maturity, the yield curve is *most likely*:
    A. flat.
    B. upward-sloping.
    C. downward sloping.

The following information relates to Questions 16–29

A one-year zero-coupon bond yields 4.0%. The two- and three-year zero-coupon bonds yield 5.0% and 6.0% respectively.

16. The rate for a one-year loan beginning in one year is *closest* to:
    A. 4.5%.
    B. 5.0%.
    C. 6.0%.
17. The forward rate for a two-year loan beginning in one year is *closest* to:
    A. 5.0%
    B. 6.0%
    C. 7.0%
18. The forward rate for a one-year loan beginning in two years is *closest* to:
    A. 6.0%
    B. 7.0%
    C. 8.0%

19. The five-year spot rate is not given above; however, the forward price for a two-year zero-coupon bond beginning in three years is known to be 0.8479. The price today of a five-year zero-coupon bond is *closest* to:
    A. 0.7119.
    B. 0.7835.
    C. 0.9524.
20. The one-year spot rate $r(1) = 4\%$, the forward rate for a one-year loan beginning in one year is 6%, and the forward rate for a one-year loan beginning in two years is 8%. Which of the following rates is *closest* to the three-year spot rate?
    A. 4.0%
    B. 6.0%
    C. 8.0%
21. The one-year spot rate $r(1) = 5\%$ and the forward price for a one-year zero-coupon bond beginning in one year is 0.9346. The spot price of a two-year zero-coupon bond is *closest* to:
    A. 0.87.
    B. 0.89.
    C. 0.93.
22. In a typical interest rate swap contract, the swap rate is *best* described as the interest rate for the:
    A. fixed-rate leg of the swap.
    B. floating-rate leg of the swap.
    C. difference between the fixed and floating legs of the swap.
23. A two-year fixed-for-floating Libor swap is 1.00% and the two-year US Treasury bond is yielding 0.63%. The swap spread is *closest* to:
    A. 37 bps.
    B. 100 bps.
    C. 163 bps.
24. The swap spread is quoted as 50 bps. If the five-year US Treasury bond is yielding 2%, the rate paid by the fixed payer in a five-year interest rate swap is *closest* to:
    A. 0.50%.
    B. 1.50%.
    C. 2.50%.
25. If the three-month T-bill rate drops and the Libor rate remains the same, the relevant TED spread:
    A. increases.
    B. decreases.
    C. does not change.
26. Given the yield curve for US Treasury zero-coupon bonds, which spread is *most* helpful pricing a corporate bond? The:
    A. Z-Spread.
    B. TED spread.
    C. Libor–OIS spread.
27. A four-year corporate bond with a 7% coupon has a Z-spread of 200 bps. Assume a flat yield curve with an interest rate for all maturities of 5% and annual compounding. The bond will *most likely* sell:
    A. close to par.
    B. at a premium to par.
    C. at a discount to par.

28. The Z-spread of Bond A is 1.05% and the Z-spread of Bond B is 1.53%. All else equal, which statement *best* describes the relationship between the two bonds?
    A. Bond B is safer and will sell at a lower price.
    B. Bond B is riskier and will sell at a lower price.
    C. Bond A is riskier and will sell at a higher price.
29. Which term structure model can be calibrated to closely fit an observed yield curve?
    A. The Ho–Lee Model
    B. The Vasicek Model
    C. The Cox–Ingersoll–Ross Model

CHAPTER 11

FIXED-INCOME PORTFOLIO MANAGEMENT—PART I

LEARNING OUTCOMES

After completing this chapter, you will be able to do the following:

- compare, with respect to investment objectives, the use of liabilities as a benchmark and the use of a bond index as a benchmark;
- compare pure bond indexing, enhanced indexing, and active investing with respect to the objectives, advantages, disadvantages, and management of each;
- discuss the criteria for selecting a benchmark bond index and justify the selection of a specific index when given a description of an investor's risk aversion, income needs, and liabilities;
- critique the use of bond market indexes as benchmarks;
- describe and evaluate techniques, such as duration matching and the use of key rate durations, by which an enhanced indexer may seek to align the risk exposures of the portfolio with those of the benchmark bond index;
- contrast and demonstrate the use of total return analysis and scenario analysis to assess the risk and return characteristics of a proposed trade;
- formulate a bond immunization strategy to ensure funding of a predetermined liability and evaluate the strategy under various interest rate scenarios;
- demonstrate the process of rebalancing a portfolio to reestablish a desired dollar duration;
- explain the importance of spread duration;
- discuss the extensions that have been made to classical immunization theory, including the introduction of contingent immunization;
- explain the risks associated with managing a portfolio against a liability structure, including interest rate risk, contingent claim risk, and cap risk;
- compare immunization strategies for a single liability, multiple liabilities, and general cash flows;
- compare risk minimization with return maximization in immunized portfolios;
- demonstrate the use of cash flow matching to fund a fixed set of future liabilities and compare the advantages and disadvantages of cash flow matching to those of immunization strategies.

SUMMARY OVERVIEW

The management of fixed-income portfolios is a highly competitive field requiring skill in financial and economic analysis, market knowledge, and control of costs. Among the points that have been made are the following:

- Because a benchmark is the standard with which the portfolio's performance will be compared, it should always reflect the portfolio's objective. If a portfolio has liabilities that must be met, that need is the paramount objective and thus is the most appropriate benchmark. If a portfolio has no liabilities, the most relevant standard is a bond market index that very closely matches the portfolio's characteristics.
- Bond indexing is attractive because indexed portfolios have lower fees than actively managed portfolios and broadly based bond index portfolios provide excellent diversification.
- In selecting a benchmark index, the manager should choose an index with comparable market value risk, comparable income risk (comparable assured income stream), and minimal liability framework risk (minimal mismatch between the durations of assets and liabilities).
- Most bond indices will not be easily replicated. Issues that prevent bond index investability include the small size of bond issues, their heterogeneity, and infrequent trading. Additionally, bond indices may have unexpected risk exposures, risk that changes over time, or be overweighted by bums. Investors may also have trouble finding an index that matches the portfolio's desired risk exposures.
- For an indexed portfolio, the manager must carefully try to match the portfolio's characteristics to the benchmark's risk profile. The primary risk factors to match are the portfolio's duration, key rate duration and cash flow distribution, sector and quality percent, sector duration contribution, quality spread duration contribution, sector/coupon/maturity/cell weights, and issuer exposure.
- The indexing manager has a variety of strategies from which to choose ranging from a totally passive style to a very active style or points in between. The most popular of these strategies are pure bond indexing, enhanced indexing by matching primary risk factors, enhanced indexing by minor risk factor mismatches, active management by larger risk factor mismatches, and full-blown active management.
- Because a perfectly indexed portfolio will still underperform the benchmark by the amount of transactions costs, the manager may use a variety of techniques to enhance the return. These include lowering managerial and transactions costs, issue selection, yield curve positioning, sector and quality positioning, and call exposure positioning.
- Total return analysis and scenario analysis are methods of evaluating the impact of a trade given a change in interest rates and a range of changes in interest rates, respectively.
- The heart of a bond immunization strategy for a single liability is to match the average duration of the assets with the time horizon of the liability. However, this matching alone is not sufficient to immunize the portfolio, in general, because of the impact of twists and nonparallel changes in the yield curve. Care must be taken when designing the immunization strategy to ensure that the portfolio will remain immunized under a variety of different scenarios.
- In order to maintain the dollar duration of a portfolio, rebalancing may be necessary. Methods for achieving this include a) investing new funds (if necessary), b) changing the weight of a particular security to adjust the dollar duration, and c) using derivatives. If new funds are invested to rebalance, after an interest rate change, calculate the new dollar duration of the portfolio, calculate the rebalancing ratio, then multiply the new market value of the portfolio by the desired percentage change.

- Spread duration is a measure of how the market value of a risky bond (portfolio) will change with respect to a parallel 100 bps change in its spread above the comparable benchmark security (portfolio). Spread duration is an important factor influencing a portfolio's total return because spreads do change frequently.
- Because parallel shifts in the yield curve are rare, classical immunization will not immunize the portfolio adequately. Extensions to classical immunization provide better results. These extensions include modifying the definition of duration (to multifunctional duration), overcoming the limitations of a fixed horizon, analyzing the risk and return trade-off for immunized portfolios, and integrating immunization strategies with elements of active bond market strategies.
- Three categories that describe the risk of not being able to pay a portfolio's liabilities are interest rate risk, contingent claim, and cap risk. A rising interest rate environment (interest rate risk) comprises the largest risk that a portfolio manager will face. When a security has a contingent claim provision, the manager may have lucrative coupon payments halted (as is the case with mortgage-backed securities) or a leveling off in the market value of a callable security. An asset that makes floating rate payments will typically have caps associated with the floating rate. The manager is at risk of the level of market rates rising while the asset returns are capped.
- Multiple liabilities immunization requires the portfolio payment stream to be decomposed so that each liability is separately immunized by one of the component streams, the present value of the assets equals the present value of the liabilities, the composite duration of the portfolio must equal the composite duration of the liabilities, and the distribution of individual portfolio assets must have a wider range than the distribution of the liabilities. For general cash flows, the expected cash contributions can be considered the payments on hypothetical securities that are part of the initial holdings. The actual initial investment can then be invested in such a way that the real and hypothetical holdings taken together represent an immunized portfolio.
- Risk minimization produces an immunized portfolio with a minimum exposure to any arbitrary interest rate change subject to the duration constraint. This objective may be too restrictive in certain situations however. If a substantial increase in the expected return can be accomplished with little effect on immunization risk, the higher-yielding portfolio may be preferred in spite of its higher risk.

PROBLEMS

Practice Problems and Solutions: 1–3 taken from from *Managing Investment Portfolios: A Dynamic Process,* Third Edition, John L. Maginn, CFA, Donald L. Tuttle, CFA, Jerald E. Pinto, CFA, and Dennis W. McLeavey, CFA, editors. Copyright © 2007 by CFA Institute. All other problems and solutions copyright © CFA Institute.

1. The table below shows the active return for six periods for a bond portfolio. Calculate the portfolio's tracking risk for the six-period time frame.

Period	Portfolio Return	Benchmark Return	Active Return
1	14.10%	13.70%	0.400%
2	8.20	8.00	0.200
3	7.80	8.00	-0.200
4	3.20	3.50	-0.300
5	2.60	2.40	0.200
6	3.30	3.00	0.300

2. The table below shows the spread duration for a 70-bond portfolio and a benchmark index based on sectors. Determine whether the portfolio or the benchmark is more sensitive to changes in the sector spread by determining the spread duration for each. Given your answer, what is the effect on the portfolio's tracking risk?

	Portfolio		Benchmark	
Sector	% of Portfolio	Spread Duration	% of Portfolio	Spread Duration
Treasury	22.70	0.00	23.10	0.00
Agencies	12.20	4.56	6.54	4.41
Financial institutions	6.23	3.23	5.89	3.35
Industrials	14.12	11.04	14.33	10.63
Utilities	6.49	2.10	6.28	2.58
Non-US credit	6.56	2.05	6.80	1.98
Mortgage	31.70	1.78	33.20	1.11
Asset backed	—	2.40	1.57	3.34
CMBS	—	5.60	2.29	4.67
Total	100.00		100.00	

3. You are the manager of a portfolio consisting of three bonds in equal par amounts of $1,000,000 each. The first table below shows the market value of the bonds and their durations. (The price includes accrued interest.) The second table contains the market value of the bonds and their durations one year later.

	Initial Values			
Security	Price	Market Value	Duration	Dollar Duration
Bond #1	$106.110	$1,060,531	5.909	?
Bond #2	98.200	981,686	3.691	?
Bond #3	109.140	1,090,797	5.843	?
		Portfolio dollar duration =		?

	After 1 Year			
Security	Price	Market Value	Duration	Dollar Duration
Bond #1	$104.240	$1,042,043	5.177	?
Bond #2	98.084	980,461	2.817	?
Bond #3	106.931	1,068,319	5.125	?
		Portfolio dollar duration =		?

As manager, you would like to maintain the portfolio's dollar duration at the initial level by rebalancing the portfolio. You choose to rebalance using the existing security proportions of one-third each. Calculate:

A. the dollar durations of each of the bonds.
B. the rebalancing ratio necessary for the rebalancing.
C. the cash required for the rebalancing.

The following information relates to Questions 4–9

The investment committee of Rojas University is unhappy with the recent performance of the fixed-income portion of their endowment and has fired the current fixed-income manager. The current portfolio, benchmarked against the Barclays Capital US Aggregate Index, is shown in Exhibit 1. The investment committee hires Alfredo Alonso, a consultant from MHC Consulting, to assess the portfolio's risks, submit ideas to the committee, and manage the portfolio on an interim basis.

EXHIBIT 1 Rojas University Endowment Fixed-Income Portfolio Information

	Portfolio		Index	
Sector	%	Duration*	%	Duration*
Treasuries	47.74	5.50	49.67	5.96
Agencies	14.79	5.80	14.79	5.10
Corporates	12.35	4.50	16.54	5.61
Mortgage-backed securities	25.12	4.65	19.10	4.65

*Spread durations are the same as effective durations for all sectors with spread risk.

Alonso notices that the fired manager's portfolio did not own securities outside of the index universe. The committee asks Alonso to consider an indexing strategy, including related benefits and logistical problems. Alonso identifies three factors that limit a manager's ability to replicate a bond index:

Factor #1 a lack of availability of certain bond issues
Factor #2 the limited market capitalization of the bond universe
Factor #3 differences between the bond prices used by the manager and the index provider

Alonso has done further analysis of the current US Treasury portion of the portfolio and has discovered a significant overweight in a 5-year Treasury bond ($10 million par value). He expects the yield curve to flatten and forecasts a six-month horizon price of the 5-year Treasury bond to be $99.50. Therefore, Alonso's strategy will be to sell all the 5-year Treasury bonds, and invest the proceeds in 10-year Treasury bonds and cash while maintaining the dollar duration of the portfolio. US Treasury bond information is shown in Exhibit 2.

EXHIBIT 2 US Treasury Bond Information

Issue Description (Term to Maturity, Ticker, Coupon, Maturity Date)	Duration	Price* ($)	Yield (%)
5-year: T 4.125% 15 May 2011	4.53	100.40625	4.03
10-year: T 5.25% 15 May 2016	8.22	109.09375	4.14

*Prices are shown per $100 par value.

4. The duration of the Rojas University fixed-income portfolio in Exhibit 1 is *closest* to:
   A. 5.11.
   B. 5.21.
   C. 5.33.
5. The spread duration of the Rojas University fixed-income portfolio in Exhibit 1 is *closest* to:
   A. 2.58.
   B. 4.93.
   C. 5.21.
6. Based on the data in Exhibit 1, the bond portfolio strategy used by the fired manager can *best* be described as:
   A. pure bond index matching.
   B. enhanced indexing/matching risk factors.
   C. active management/larger risk factor mismatches.
7. Regarding the three factors identified by Alonso, the factor *least likely* to actually limit a manager's ability to replicate a bond index is:
   A. #1.
   B. #2.
   C. #3.
8. Using Alonso's forecasted price and the bond information in Exhibit 2, the expected 6-month total return of the Treasury 4.125% 15 May 2011 is *closest* to (assume zero accrued interest at purchase):
   A. -0.90%.
   B. 1.15%.
   C. 1.56%.
9. Using Exhibit 2, the par value of 10-year bonds to be purchased to execute Alonso's strategy is *closest* to:
   A. $5,072,000.
   B. $5,489,000.
   C. $5,511,000.

The following information relates to Questions 10–15

The State Retirement Board (SRB) provides a defined benefit pension plan to state employees. The governors of the SRB are concerned that their current fixed-income investments may not be appropriate because the average age of the state employee workforce has been increasing. In addition, a surge in retirements is projected to occur over the next 10 years.

Chow Wei Mei, the head of the SRB's investment committee, has suggested that some of the future pension payments can be covered by buying annuities from an insurance company. She proposes that the SRB invest a fixed sum to purchase annuities in seven years time, when the number of retirements is expected to peak. Chow argues that the SRB should fund the future purchase of the annuities by creating a dedicated fixed-income portfolio consisting of corporate bonds, mortgage-backed securities, and risk-free government bonds. Chow states:

Statement #1 "To use a portfolio of bonds to immunize a single liability, and remove all risks, it is necessary only that 1) the market value of the assets be equal to the present value of the liability and 2) the duration of the portfolio be equal to the duration of the liability."

Chow lists three alternative portfolios that she believes will immunize a single, seven-year liability. All bonds in Exhibit 1 are option-free government bonds.

EXHIBIT 1 Alternative Portfolios for F.unding an Annuity Purchase in Seven Years

Portfolio	Description	Portfolio Yield to Maturity (%)
A	Zero-coupon bond with a maturity of 7 years	4.20
B	Bond with a maturity of 6 years Bond with a maturity of 8 years	4.10
C	Bond with a maturity of 5 years Bond with a maturity of 9 years	4.15

Chow then states:

Statement #2 "Because each of these alternative portfolios immunizes this single, seven-year liability, each has the same level of reinvestment risk."

The SRB governors would like to examine different investment horizons and alternative strategies to immunize the single liability. The governors ask Chow to evaluate a contingent immunization strategy using the following assumptions:

- The SRB will commit a $100 million investment to this strategy.
- The horizon of the investment is 10 years.
- The SRB will accept a 4.50 percent return (semiannual compounding).
- An immunized rate of return of 5.25 percent (semiannual compounding) is possible.

Marshall Haley, an external consultant for the SRB, has been asked by the governors to advise them on the appropriateness of its investment strategies. Haley notes that, although state employee retirements are expected to surge over the next 10 years, the SRB will experience a continual stream of retirements over the next several decades. Hence, the SRB faces a schedule of liabilities, not a single liability. In explaining how the SRB can manage the risks of multiple liabilities, Haley makes the following statements:

Statement #1 "When managing the risks of a schedule of liabilities, multiple liability immunization and cash flow matching approaches do not have the same risks and costs. Whereas cash flow matching generally has less risk of not satisfying future liabilities, multiple liability immunization generally costs less."

Statement #2 "Assuming that there is a parallel shift in the yield curve, to immunize multiple liabilities, there are three necessary conditions: i) the present value of the assets be equal to the present value of the liabilities; ii) the composite portfolio duration be equal to the composite liabilities duration; and iii) I cannot remember the third condition."

Statement #3 "Horizon matching can be used to immunize a schedule of liabilities."

10. Is Chow's Statement #1 correct?
    A. Yes.
    B. No, because credit risk must also be considered.
    C. No, because the risk of parallel shifts in the yield curve must also be considered.

11. Is Chow's Statement #2 correct?
    A. No, Portfolio B is exposed to less reinvestment risk than Portfolio A.
    B. No, Portfolio B is exposed to more reinvestment risk than Portfolio C.
    C. No, Portfolio C is exposed to more reinvestment risk than Portfolio B.
12. Which of the following is *closest* to the required terminal value for the contingent immunization strategy?
    A. $100 million.
    B. $156 million.
    C. $168 million.
13. Is Haley's Statement #1 correct?
    A. Yes.
    B. No, because multiple liability immunization is generally less risky than cash flow matching.
    C. No, because cash flow matching is generally less costly than multiple liability immunization.
14. The condition that Haley cannot remember in his Statement #2 is that the:
    A. cash flows in the portfolio must be dispersed around the horizon date.
    B. cash flows in the portfolio must be concentrated around the horizon date.
    C. distribution of durations of individual assets in the portfolio must have a wider range than the distribution of the liabilities.
15. The *most* appropriate description of the strategy that Haley suggests in his Statement #3 is to create a portfolio that:
    A. has cash flows concentrated around the horizon date.
    B. is duration matched but uses cash flow matching in the later years of the liability schedule.
    C. is duration matched but uses cash flow matching in the initial years of the liability schedule.

CHAPTER 12

FIXED-INCOME PORTFOLIO MANAGEMENT—PART II

LEARNING OUTCOMES

After completing this chapter, you will be able to do the following:

- evaluate the effect of leverage on portfolio duration and investment returns;
- discuss the use of repurchase agreements (repos) to finance bond purchases and the factors that affect the repo rate;
- critique the use of standard deviation, target semivariance, shortfall risk, and value at risk as measures of fixed-income portfolio risk;
- demonstrate the advantages of using futures instead of cash market instruments to alter portfolio risk;
- formulate and evaluate an immunization strategy based on interest rate futures;
- explain the use of interest rate swaps and options to alter portfolio cash flows and exposure to interest rate risk;
- compare default risk, credit spread risk, and downgrade risk and demonstrate the use of credit derivative instruments to address each risk in the context of a fixed-income portfolio;
- explain the potential sources of excess return for an international bond portfolio;
- evaluate 1) the change in value for a foreign bond when domestic interest rates change and 2) the bond's contribution to duration in a domestic portfolio, given the duration of the foreign bond and the country beta;
- recommend and justify whether to hedge or not hedge currency risk in an international bond investment;
- describe how breakeven spread analysis can be used to evaluate the risk in seeking yield advantages across international bond markets;
- discuss the advantages and risks of investing in emerging market debt;
- discuss the criteria for selecting a fixed-income manager.

SUMMARY OVERVIEW

The management of fixed-income portfolios is a highly competitive field requiring skill in financial and economic analysis, market knowledge, and control of costs. Among the points that have been made are the following:

- Standard deviation, target semivariance, shortfall risk, and value at risk have all been proposed as appropriate measures of risk for a portfolio. However, each has its own deficiency. For example, standard deviation (or variance) assumes that risk has a normal distribution (which may not be true). Semivariance often provides little extra information if returns are symmetric. Shortfall risk is expressed as a probability, not as a currency amount. Value at risk does not indicate the magnitude of the very worst possible outcomes.
- A repurchase agreement is subject to a variety of credit risks, including:
  a. *Quality of the collateral.* The higher the quality of the securities, the lower the repo rate will be.
  b. *Term of the repo.* Typically, the longer the maturity, the higher the rate will be.
  c. *Delivery requirement.* If physical delivery of the securities is required, the rate will be lower because of the lower credit risk.
  d. *Availability of collateral.* The buyer of the securities may be willing to accept a lower rate in order to obtain securities that are in short supply.
  e. *Prevailing interest rates in the economy.* As interest rates increase, the rates on repo transactions will generally increase.
  f. *Seasonal factors.* A seasonal effect may exist because some institutions' supply of funds varies by the season.
- The primary advantages to using futures to alter a portfolio's duration are increased liquidity and cost-effectiveness.
- Futures contracts can be used to shorten or lengthen a portfolio's duration. The contracts may also be used to hedge or reduce an existing interest rate exposure. As such, they may be combined with traditional immunization techniques to improve the results.
- Unlike ordinary bond options that protect against interest rate risk, credit options are structured to offer protection against credit risk. Binary credit option and binary credit option based on a credit rating are the two types of credit options written on an underlying asset. The former pays the option buyer in the event of default; otherwise nothing is paid. The latter pays the difference between the strike price and the market price when the specified credit rating event occurs and pays nothing if the event does not occur.
- Credit options are structured to offer protection against both default risk and credit spread risk, credit forwards offer protection against credit spread risk, and credit default swaps help in managing default risk.
- The sources of excess return for an international bond portfolio include bond market selection, currency selection, duration management/yield curve management, sector selection, credit analysis, and investing in markets outside the benchmark index.
- Emerging market debt has matured as an asset class. The spread of EMD over risk-free rates has narrowed considerably as the quality of sovereign bonds has increased to the point that they now have similar frequencies of default, recovery rates, and ratings transition probabilities compared with corporate bonds with similar ratings.
- Emerging market debt is still risky, however, and is characterized by high volatility and returns that exhibit significant negative skewness. Moreover, emerging market countries frequently do not offer the degree of transparency, court tested laws, and clear regulations found in established markets.

- For a change in domestic interest rates, the change in a foreign bond's value may be found by multiplying the duration of the foreign bond times the country beta. Because a portfolio's duration is a weighted average of the duration of the bonds in the portfolio, the contribution to the portfolio's duration is equal to the adjusted foreign bond duration multiplied by its weight in the portfolio.
- Breakeven spread analysis is used to estimate relative values between markets by quantifying the amount of spread widening required to reduce a foreign bond's yield advantage to zero. The breakeven spread can be found by dividing the yield advantage by the bond's duration.
- When funds are not managed entirely in-house, a search for outside managers must be conducted. The due diligence for selection of managers is satisfied primarily by investigating the managers' investment process, the types of trades the managers are making, and the organizational strengths.

PROBLEMS

Practice Problems and Solutions 1–10 and 29 taken from *Managing Investment Portfolios: A Dynamic Process,* Third Edition, John L. Maginn, CFA, Donald L. Tuttle, CFA, Jerald E. Pinto, CFA, and Dennis W. McLeavey, CFA, editors. Copyright © 2007 by CFA Institute. All other problems and solutions copyright © CFA Institute.

1. Your client has asked you to construct a £2 million bond portfolio. Some of the bonds that you are considering for this portfolio have embedded options. Your client has specified that he may withdraw £25,000 from the portfolio in six months to fund some expected expenses. He would like to be able to make this withdrawal without reducing the initial capital of £2 million.
   A. Would shortfall risk be an appropriate measure of risk while evaluating the portfolios for your client?
   B. What are some of the shortcomings of the use of shortfall risk?
2. The market value of the bond portfolio of a French investment fund is €75 million. The duration of the portfolio is 8.17. Based on the analysis provided by the in-house economists, the portfolio manager believes that the interest rates are likely to have an unexpected decrease over the next month. Based on this belief, the manager has decided to increase the duration of its entire bond portfolio to 10. The futures contract it would use is priced at €130,000 and has a duration of 9.35. Assume that the conversion factor for the futures contract is 1.06.
   A. Would the fund need to buy futures contracts or sell?
   B. Approximately, how many futures contracts would be needed to change the duration of the bond portfolio?
3. The trustees of a pension fund would like to examine the issue of protecting the bonds in the fund's portfolio against an increase in interest rates using options and futures. Before discussing this with their external bond fund manager, they decide to ask four consultants about their recommendations as to what should be done at this time. It turns out that each of them has a different recommendation. Consultant A suggests selling covered calls, Consultant B suggests doing nothing at all, Consultant C suggests selling interest rate futures, and Consultant D suggests buying puts. The reason for their different recommendations is that although all consultants understand the pension fund's objective of minimizing risk, they differ with one another in regards to their outlook on future interest rates. One of the consultants believes interest rates are headed downward, one has no opinion, one believes that the interest rates would not change much in either direction,

and one believes that the interest rates are headed upward. Based on the consultants' recommendations, could you identify the outlook of each consultant?

4. The current credit spread on bonds issued by Great Foods Inc. is 300 bps. The manager of More Money Funds believes that Great Foods' credit situation will improve over the next few months, resulting in a smaller credit spread on its bonds. She decides to enter into a six-month credit spread forward contract taking the position that the credit spread will decrease. The forward contract has the current spread as the contracted spread, a notional amount of $10 million, and a risk factor of 5.
   A. On the settlement date six months later, the credit spread on Great Foods bonds is 250 bps. How much is the payoff to More Money Funds?
   B. How much would the payoff to More Money Funds be if the credit spread on the settlement date is 350 bps?
   C. How much is the maximum possible gain for More Money Funds?
5. Consider a collateralized debt obligation (CDO) that has a $250 million structure. The collateral consists of bonds that mature in seven years, and the coupon rate for these bonds is the seven-year Treasury rate plus 500 bps. The senior tranche comprises 70 percent of the structure and has a floating coupon of Libor plus 50 bps. There is only one junior tranche that comprises 20 percent of the structure and has a fixed coupon of seven-year Treasury rate plus 300 bps. Compute the rate of return earned by the equity tranche in this CDO if the seven-year Treasury rate is 6 percent and the Libor is 7.5 percent. There are no defaults in the underlying collateral pool. Ignore the collateral manager's fees and any other expenses.
6. Assume that the rates shown in the table below accurately reflect current conditions in the financial markets.

Dollar/Euro Spot Rate	1.21
Dollar/Euro 1-Year Forward Rate	1.18
1-Year Deposit Rate:	
Euro	3%
US	2%

   In the table, the one-year forward dollar/euro exchange rate is mispriced, because it doesn't reflect the interest rate differentials between the United States and Europe.
   A. Calculate the amount of the current forward exchange discount or premium.
   B. Calculate the value that the forward rate would need to be in order to keep riskless arbitrage from occurring.
7. Assume that a US bond investor has invested in Canadian government bonds. The duration of a 12-year Canadian government bond is 8.40, and the Canadian country beta is 0.63. Interest rates in the United States are expected to change by approximately 80 bps. How much can the US investor expect the Canadian bond to change in value if US rates change by 80 bps?
8. Assume that the spread between US and German bonds is 300 bps, providing German investors who purchase a US bond with an additional yield income of 75 bps per quarter. The duration of the German bond is 8.3. If German interest rates should decline, how much of a decline is required to completely wipe out the quarterly yield advantage for the German investor?
9. A portfolio manager of a Canadian fund that invests in the yen-denominated Japanese bonds is considering whether or not to hedge the portfolio's exposure to the Japanese

yen using a forward contract. Assume that the short-term interest rates are 1.6 percent in Japan and 2.7 percent in Canada.

A. Based on the in-house analysis provided by the fund's currency specialists, the portfolio manager expects the Japanese yen to appreciate against the Canadian dollar by 1.5 percent. Should the portfolio manager hedge the currency risk using a forward contract?

B. What would be your answer if the portfolio manager expects the Japanese yen to appreciate against the Canadian dollar by only 0.5 percent?

10. A British fixed-income fund has substantial holdings in US dollar-denominated bonds. The fund's portfolio manager is considering whether to leave the fund's exposure to the US dollar unhedged or to hedge it using a UK pound–US dollar forward contract. Assume that the short-term interest rates are 4.7 percent in the United Kingdom and 4 percent in the United States. The fund manager expects the US dollar to appreciate against the pound by 0.4 percent. Assume IRP holds. Explain which alternative has the higher expected return based on the short-term interest rates and the manager's expectations about exchange rates.

The following information relates to Questions 11–16

Sheila Ibahn, a portfolio manager with TBW Incorporated, is reviewing the performance of L.P. Industries' $100 million fixed-income portfolio with Stewart Palme from L.P. Industries. TBW Incorporated employs an active management strategy for fixed-income portfolios. Ibahn explains to Palme that the portfolio return was greater than the benchmark return last year and states:

> "We outperformed our benchmark by using inter-sector allocation and individual security selection strategies rather than a duration management strategy. However, at this point in the interest rate cycle, we believe we can add relative return by taking on additional interest rate risk across the portfolio."

Ibahn recommends purchasing additional bonds to adjust the average duration of the portfolio. After reviewing the portfolio recommendations, Palme asks Ibahn:

> "How can we adjust the portfolio's duration without contributing significant funds to purchase additional bonds in the portfolio?"

Ibahn responds:

Ibahn 1	We could employ futures contracts to adjust the duration of the portfolio, thus eliminating the need to purchase more bonds.
Ibahn 2	We could lever the portfolio by entering into either an overnight or 2-year term repurchase agreement [repo] and use the repo funds to purchase additional bonds that have the same duration as the current portfolio. For example, if we use funds from a $25 million overnight repo agreement to purchase bonds in addition to the current $100 million portfolio, the levered portfolio's change in value for a 1% change in interest rates would equal $5,125,000 while giving you the portfolio duration you require. Unfortunately the current cost of the repo is high because the repo collateral is "special collateral" but the margin requirement is low because the collateral is illiquid.

After listening to Ibahn, Palme agrees to use a repo to lever the portfolio but leaves the repo term decision to Ibahn's discretion. Because the yield curve is inverted, the cost of both the overnight and the 2-year term repo is higher than the yield on the levered portfolio. As Ibahn and Palme discuss the repo term, Palme asks two final questions:

Palme 1	"What is the effect of leverage on a portfolio's range of returns if interest rates are expected to change?"
Palme 2	"If interest rates are unchanged over a six-month period, what is the effect on the levered portfolio return compared to the unlevered portfolio return?"

11. Given Ibahn's recommendation, which of the following interest rate forecasts is TBW Incorporated *most likely* using?
    A. A flattening of the yield curve.
    B. An upward parallel shift in the yield curve.
    C. A downward parallel shift in the yield curve.
12. Referring to Ibahn's first response to Palme, which of the following best describes TBW's *most likely* course of action?
    A. Sell interest rate futures contracts to increase portfolio duration.
    B. Buy interest rate futures contracts to increase portfolio duration.
    C. Buy interest rate futures contracts to decrease portfolio duration.
13. Referring to Ibahn's second response to Palme, the levered portfolio would have:
    A. the same duration if either the overnight repo or the 2-year term repo is used.
    B. a longer duration if the overnight repo is used instead of the 2-year term repo.
    C. a shorter duration if the overnight repo is used instead of the 2-year term repo.
14. In Ibahn's second response to Palme, the duration of the sample leveraged portfolio is *closest* to:
    A. 4.10.
    B. 5.13.
    C. 6.83.
15. Is Ibahn's second response to Palme regarding the cost and margin requirements for the repo *most likely* correct?

	High Repo Cost	Low Margin Requirement
A.	No	No
B.	Yes	Yes
C.	Yes	No

16. In response to Palme's two final questions, the levered portfolio's range of returns and six-month return when compared to the unlevered portfolio *most likely* would be:

	Levered Portfolio Range of Returns	Levered Portfolio Six-month Return
A.	narrower	lower
B.	narrower	higher
C.	wider	lower

The following information relates to Questions 17–22 and is based on "Fixed-Income Portfolio Management—Part I" and this chapter

The investment committee of the US-based Autónoma Foundation has been dissatisfied with the performance of the fixed-income portion of their endowment and has recently fired the fixed-income manager.

The investment committee has hired a consultant, Julia Santillana, to oversee the portfolio on an interim basis until the search for a new manager is completed. She is also expected to assess the portfolio's risks and propose investment ideas to the committee.

Total Return Analysis and Scenario Analysis

During a meeting between Santillana and members of the committee, a member asks her to discuss the use of total return analysis and scenario analysis before executing bond trades. In her response, Santillana states:

- "To compute total return, the manager needs a set of assumptions about the investment horizon, the expected reinvestment rate, and the expected change in interest rates."
- "If the manager wants to evaluate how the individual assumptions affect the total return computation, she can use scenario analysis."
- "Scenario analysis can lead to rejection of a strategy that is acceptable from a total return perspective."

Use of Repurchase Agreements

During the meeting, Santillana reviews with the investment committee a hypothetical transaction in which leverage is used. A manager with $2 million of funds to invest purchases corporate bonds with a market value of $7 million. To partially finance the purchase, the manager enters into a 30-day repurchase agreement with the bond dealer for $5 million. The 30-day term repo rate is assumed to be 4.20 percent per year. At the end of the 30 days, when the transaction expires, the corporate bonds are assumed to have increased in value by 0.30 percent. Santillana uses this information to demonstrate the effects of leverage on portfolio returns.

Responding to a question asked by a committee member, Santillana explains: "The quality of collateral as well as short sellers' positions affect the repo rate."

International Bond Investing and Hedging

Santillana also mentions to the investment committee that the Foundation's current portfolio does not include international bonds. She describes the benefits of investing in international bonds and answers the committee's questions. Exhibit 1 displays information she uses during the meeting to clarify her answers. The 1-year interest rate is used as a proxy for the risk-free rate.

EXHIBIT 1 Summary Information Relevant to International Bond Investing

	UK	Japan	Germany	Singapore	US
1-year interest rate (percent)	6.24	0.97	4.69	2.09	5.30
Yield on 10-year government bond/note (percent)	5.04	1.67	4.36	2.74	4.62
Expected one-year currency appreciation in percent (USD per local currency)	0.10	0.50	0.95	1.60	N/A
10-year bond duration	7.34	9.12	7.72	8.19	7.79

The committee is persuaded by Santillana's presentation and decides to invest in international bonds. As a result, Santillana considers whether she should recommend currency hedging using forward contracts, assuming that interest rate parity holds.

During the discussion on international bond investing, a member comments that investors in Japan and Singapore in particular should be investing in the United States because of the difference in bond yields. Santillana agrees but explains that investors should also perform a breakeven spread analysis when investing internationally.

17. Is Santillana correct in her statements about total return analysis *and* scenario analysis?
    A. Yes.
    B. No, because scenario analysis cannot evaluate how individual assumptions affect the total return computation.
    C. No, because scenario analysis cannot lead to a rejection of a strategy with an acceptable expected total return.
18. The 30-day rate of return on the hypothetical leveraged portfolio of corporate bonds is *closest* to:
    A. –0.05 percent.
    B. 0.05 percent.
    C. 0.18 percent.
19. Is Santillana correct in her explanation of factors affecting the repo rate?
    A. Yes.
    B. No, only the quality of collateral is correct.
    C. No, only the short sellers' position is correct.
20. Based on Exhibit 1 and assuming interest rates remain unchanged, which bond will have the *highest* hedged return?
    A. UK 10-year.
    B. Japan 10-year.
    C. Germany 10-year.
21. Based on Exhibit 1 and assuming interest rates remain unchanged, which bond will have the *highest* expected unhedged return?
    A. UK 10-year.
    B. Germany 10-year.
    C. Singapore 10-year.
22. Based on Exhibit 1, for investors that purchased 10-year US notes, the spread widening in basis points that will wipe out the additional yield gained for a quarter is *closest* to:
    A. 6.03 in Singapore.
    B. 8.09 in Japan.
    C. 13.48 in the United Kingdom.

The following information relates to Questions 23–28 and is based on "Fixed-Income Portfolio Management—Part I" and this chapter

Salvatore Choo, the Chief Investment Officer at European Pension Fund (EPF), wishes to maintain the fixed-income portfolio's active management but recognizes that the portfolio must remain fully funded. The portfolio is run by World Asset Management, where Jimmy Ferragamo, a risk manager, is analyzing the portfolio (shown in Exhibit 1), whose benchmark has a duration of 5.6. None of the bonds in the portfolio have embedded options. However, EPF's liability has a duration of 10.2, creating an asset liability mismatch for the pension fund.

EXHIBIT 1 EPF Portfolio

Maturity	Market Value (000)	Duration
2-year bond	€421,000	1.8
5-year bond	€1,101,000	4.8
10-year bond	€1,540,000	8.4
Total	€3,062,000	6.2

Choo is utilizing a contingent immunization (CI) approach to achieve better returns for the fund, so by his understanding of CI, he can use the entire fixed-income portfolio for active management until the portfolio drops below the safety net level or the terminal value.

Ferragamo runs the following risk statistics on the EPF portfolio to ensure that they are not outside the EPF trustee guidelines. He has the following comment:

> "The portfolio value at risk, as opposed to shortfall risk and standard deviation, determines the most the portfolio can lose in any month."

Ferragamo has collected the following data on the bund (German Bond) future, which has a conversion factor of 1.1, and the cheapest to deliver bond is priced at €100,000 and has a duration of 8.2.

In addition to his CIO responsibilities, Choo is also responsible for managing the funding liabilities for a new wing at the local hospital, which is currently fully funded utilizing a standard immunization approach with noncallable bonds. However, he is concerned about the various risks associated with the liabilities including interest rate risk, contingent claim risk, and cap risk.

Choo is interested in using cash flow matching rather than immunization to fund a liability for the new wing. The liability is denominated in euros and will be a lump sum payment in five years. The term structure of interest rates is currently a steep upward-sloping yield curve.

23. Given the term structure of interest rates and the duration mismatch between EPF's benchmark and its pension liability, the plan should be *most concerned* about a:
    A. flattening of the yield curve.
    B. steepening of the yield curve.
    C. large parallel shift up in the yield curve.
24. Choo's understanding of contingent immunization (CI) is:
    A. correct.
    B. incorrect, because CI does not use a terminal value.
    C. incorrect, because CI does not allow for active management.
25. Is Ferragamo's comment correct?
    A. Yes.
    B. No, because shortfall risk would provide this information.
    C. No, because value at risk does not indicate the magnitude of the very worst possible outcomes.
26. Based on the data Ferragamo collected on the bund and Exhibit 1, Choo can adjust the EPF portfolio duration to match the benchmark duration by selling:
    A. 2,240 contracts.
    B. 2,406 contracts.
    C. 2,465 contracts.

27. Are Choo's concerns regarding various risks of funding the hospital liability correct?
    A. Yes.
    B. No, because interest rate risk is not a factor.
    C. No, because contingent claim risk is not a factor.
28. Which of the following would best immunize the hospital liability?
    A. A five-year euro coupon bond.
    B. A five-year euro zero-coupon bond.
    C. Equal investment in three- and seven-year euro zero-coupon bonds.

The following problem is based on "Fixed-Income Portfolio Management—Part I" and this chapter

29. A portfolio manager decided to purchase corporate bonds with a market value of €5 million. To finance 60 percent of the purchase, the portfolio manager entered into a 30-day repurchase agreement with the bond dealer. The 30-day term repo rate was 4.6 percent per year. At the end of the 30 days, the bonds purchased by the portfolio manager have increased in value by 0.5 percent and the portfolio manager decided to sell the bonds. No coupons were received during the 30-day period.
    A. Compute the 30-day rate of return on the equity and borrowed components of the portfolio.
    B. Compute the 30-day portfolio rate of return.
    C. Compute the 30-day portfolio rate of return if the increase in value of the bonds was 0.3 percent instead of 0.5 percent.
    D. Use your answers to parts B and C above to comment on the effect of the use of leverage on the portfolio rate of return.
    E. Discuss why the bond dealer in the above example faces a credit risk even if the bond dealer holds the collateral.

CHAPTER 13

RELATIVE-VALUE METHODOLOGIES FOR GLOBAL CREDIT BOND PORTFOLIO MANAGEMENT

LEARNING OUTCOMES

After completing this chapter, you will be able to do the following:

- explain classic relative-value analysis, based on top-down and bottom-up approaches to credit bond portfolio management;
- discuss the implications of cyclical supply and demand changes in the primary corporate bond market and the impact of secular changes in the market's dominant product structures;
- explain the influence of investors' short- and long-term liquidity needs on portfolio management decisions;
- discuss common rationales for secondary market trading;
- discuss corporate bond portfolio strategies that are based on relative value.

SUMMARY OVERVIEW

- Superior credit analysis has been and will remain the most important determinant of the relative performance of credit bond portfolios, allowing managers to identify potential credit upgrades and to avoid potential downgrades.
- The "corporate asset class" includes more than pure corporate entities; this segment of the global bond market is more properly called the "credit asset class," including sovereigns, supranationals, agencies of local government authorities, nonagency mortgage-backed securities, commercial mortgage-backed securities, and asset-backed securities.
- Relative value refers to the ranking of fixed-income investments by sectors, structures, issuers, and issues in terms of their expected performance during some future interval.
- Relative-value analysis refers to the methodologies used to generate expected return rankings.

- Within the global credit market, classic relative-value analysis combines top-down and bottom-up approaches, blending the macro input of chief investment officers, strategists, economists, and portfolio managers with the micro input of credit analysts, quantitative analysts, and portfolio managers.
- The objective of relative value analysis is to identify the sectors with the most potential upside, populate these favored sectors with the best representative issuers, and select the structures of the designated issuers at the yield curve points that match the investor's outlook for the benchmark yield curve.
- The main methodologies for credit relative-value maximization are total return analysis, primary market analysis, liquidity and trading analysis, secondary trading rationales and constraints analysis, spread analysis, structure analysis, credit curve analysis, credit analysis, and asset allocation/sector analysis.
- Credit relative-value analysis starts with a detailed decomposition of past returns and a projection of expected returns.
- Primary market analysis refers to analyzing the supply and demand for new issues.
- The global credit market has become structurally more homogeneous, with intermediate maturity (5 to 10 years) bullet structure (noncallable issues) coming to dominate the investment-grade market.
- The trend toward bullet securities does not pertain to the high-yield market, where callable structures dominate the market.
- Short-term and long-term liquidity influence portfolio management decisions.
- Credit market liquidity changes over time, varying with the economic cycle, credit cycle, shape of the yield curve, supply, and the season.
- Despite the limitations of yield measures, yield/spread pickup trades account for the most common secondary market trades across all sectors of the global credit market.
- Credit-upside trades seek to capitalize on expectations of issues that will be upgraded in credit quality with such trades particularly popular in the crossover sector (securities with ratings between Ba2/BB and Baa3/BBB– by a major rating agency).
- Credit-defense trades involve trading up in credit quality as economic or geopolitical uncertainty increases.
- Sector-rotation trades involve altering allocations among sectors based on relative-value analysis; such strategies can be used within the credit bond market (intra-asset class sector rotation) and among fixed-income asset classes.
- Sector-rotation trades are not as popular in the bond market as in the equity market because of less liquidity and higher costs of trading; however, with the expected development of enhanced liquidity and lower trading transaction costs in the future, sector-rotation trades should become more prevalent in the credit asset class.
- Trades undertaken to reposition a portfolio's duration are called yield curve-adjustment trades, or simply, curve-adjustment trades.
- Structure trades involve swaps into structures (e.g., callable structures, bullet structures, and put structures) that are expected to have better performance given anticipated movements in volatility and the shape of the yield curve.
- Portfolio managers should review their main rationales for not trading.
- Portfolio constraints are the single biggest contributor to the persistence of market inefficiency across the global credit bond market.
- Many US practitioners prefer to cast the valuations of investment-grade credit securities in terms of option-adjusted spreads (OAS), but given the rapid reduction of credit structures

with embedded options since 1990, the use of OAS in primary and secondary pricing has diminished within the investment-grade credit asset class.

- Swap spreads have become a popular valuation yardstick for European credit, Asian credit, and US MBS, CMBS, agency, and ABS sectors.
- In the global credit bond market, nominal spread (the yield difference between credit and government bonds of similar maturities) has been the basic unit of relative-value analysis.
- Mean-reversion analysis is the most common technique for analyzing spreads among individual securities and across industry sectors.
- Mean-reversion analysis can be misleading because the mean or average value is highly dependent on the time period analyzed.
- In quality-spread analysis, a manager examines the spread differentials between low- and high-quality credits.
- Structural analysis involves analyzing different structures' performance on a relative-value basis.
- Put structures provide investors with a partial defense against sharp increases in interest rates: this structure should be favored as an outperformance vehicle only by those investors with a decidedly bearish outlook for interest rates.
- Credit curves, both term structure and credit structure, are almost always positively sloped.
- In credit barbell strategies, many portfolio managers choose to take credit risk in short and intermediate maturities and to substitute less risky government securities in long-duration portfolio buckets.
- Like the underlying Treasury benchmark curve, credit spread curves change shape over the course of economic cycles; typically, spread curves steepen when the bond market becomes more wary of interest rate and general credit risk.

PROBLEMS

Practice Problems and Solutions 1–20 taken from *Fixed Income Readings for the Chartered Financial Analyst® Program*, Second Edition, edited by Frank J. Fabozzi, CFA. Copyright © 2005 by CFA Institute. All other problems and solutions copyright © CFA Institute.

1. What is meant by relative value in the credit market?
2. A. What is the dominant type of structure in the investment-grade credit market?
   B. What are the strategic portfolio implications of the dominant structure answer in Part (A)?
   C. What is the dominant structure in the high-yield corporate bond market and why is it not the same structure as discussed in Part (A)?
3. The following quote is from Lev Dynkin, Peter Ferket, Jay Hyman, Erik van Leeuwen, and Wei Wu, "Value of Security Selection versus Asset Allocation in Credit Markets," Fixed Income Research, Lehman Brothers, March 1999, p. 3:

   > Most fixed income investors in the United States have historically remained in a single-currency world. Their efforts to outperform their benchmarks have focused on yield curve placement, sector and quality allocations, and security selection. The style of market participants is expressed in the amount of risk assumed along each of these dimensions (as measured by the deviation from their benchmarks), and their research efforts are directed accordingly.

A. What is meant by "yield curve placement, sector and quality allocations, and security selection"?
B. What is meant by the statement: "The style of market participants is expressed in the amount of risk assumed along each of these dimensions (as measured by the deviation from their benchmarks)"?

4. The following two passages are from Peter J. Carril, "Relative Value Concepts within the Eurobond Market," Chapter 29 in Frank J. Fabozzi (ed.), *The Handbook of Corporate Debt Instruments* (New Hope, PA: Frank J. Fabozzi Associates, 1998), p. 552.
   A. In discussing Eurobond issuers, Carril wrote: "Many first time issuers produce tighter spreads than one may anticipate because of their so called scarcity value." What is meant by scarcity value?
   B. In describing putable bonds Carril wrote: "Much analytical work has been devoted to the valuation of the put's option value, especially in the more mature US investment-grade market." However, he states that in the high-yield market the overriding concern for a putable issue is one of credit concern. Specifically, he wrote: "traditional analysis used to quantify the option value which the issuer has granted the investor is overridden by the investor's specific view of the credit-worthiness of the issuer at the time of first put." Explain why.
5. In describing the approaches to investing in emerging markets credits, Christopher Taylor wrote the following in "Challenges in the Credit Analysis of Emerging Market Corporate Bonds," Chapter 16 in Frank J. Fabozzi (ed.), *The Handbook of Corporate Debt Instruments* (New Hope, PA: Frank J. Fabozzi Associates, 1998), p. 311:

   > There traditionally have been two approaches to investing in emerging market corporate bonds: top-down and bottom-up. . . . The *top-down approach* essentially treats investing in corporates as "sovereign-plus." The *bottom-up approach* sometimes has a tendency to treat emerging market corporate as "US credits-plus."

   What do you think Mr. Taylor means by "sovereign-plus" and "US credits-plus"?
6. Chris Dialynas in "The Active Decisions in the Selection of Passive Management and Performance Bogeys" (in Frank J. Fabozzi (ed.), *Perspectives on Fixed Income Portfolio Management,* Volume 2) wrote:

   > Active bond managers each employ their own methods for relative value analysis. Common elements among most managers are historical relations, liquidity considerations, and market segmentation. Market segmentation allegedly creates opportunities, and historical analysis provides the timing cure.

   A. What is meant by "historical relations, liquidity considerations, and market segmentation" that Chris Dialynas refers to in this passage?
   B. What is meant by: "Market segmentation allegedly creates opportunities, and historical analysis provides the timing cure?"
7. The following passages are from Leland Crabbe "Corporate Spread Curve Strategies," Chapter 28 in Frank J. Fabozzi (ed.), *The Handbook of CorporateDebt Instruments* (New Hope, PA: Frank J. Fabozzi Associates, 1998).

   > In the corporate bond market, spread curves often differ considerably across issuers . . .

> Most fixed income investors understand the relation between the term structure of interest rates and implied forward rates. But some investors overlook the fact that a similar relation holds between the term structure of corporate spreads and forward corporate spreads. Specifically, when the spread curve is steep, the forward spreads imply that spreads will widen over time. By contrast, a flat spread curve gives rise to forwards that imply stability in corporate spreads. Essentially the forward spread can be viewed as a breakeven spread . . .
>
> Sometimes, investors may disagree with the expectations implied by forward rates, and consequently they may want to implement trading strategies to profit from reshapings of the spread curve.

A. What is meant by "spread curves" and in what ways do they differ across issuers?
B. Consider the relationship between the term structure of interest rates and implied forward rates (or simply forward rates). What is a "forward spread" that Mr. Crabbe refers to and why can it be viewed as a breakeven spread?
C. How can implied forward spreads be used in relative-value analysis?

8. What is the limitation of a yield-pickup trade?
9. Increases in investment-grade credit securities new issuance have been observed with contracting yield spreads and strong relative bond returns. In contrast, spread expansion and a major decline in both relative and absolute returns usually accompanies a sharp decline in the supply of new credit issues. These outcomes are in stark contrast to the conventional wisdom held by many portfolio managers that supply hurts credit spreads. What reason can be offered for the observed relationship between new supply and changes in credit spreads?
10. A. What is meant by the "crossover sector of the bond market"?
    B. How do portfolio managers take advantage of potential credit upgrades in the crossover sector?
11. When would a portfolio manager consider implementing a credit-defense trade?
12. What is the motivation for portfolio managers to trade into more current and larger sized "on-the-run" issues?
13. A. Why has the swap spread framework become a popular valuation yardstick in Europe for credit securities?
    B. Why might US managers embrace the swap spread framework for the credit asset class?
    C. Compare the advantages/disadvantage of the nominal spread framework to the swap spread framework.
14. An ABC Corporate issue trades at a bid price of 120 bps over the 5-year US Treasury yield of 6.00% at a time when Libor is 5.70%. At the same time, 5-year Libor-based swap spreads equal 100 bps (to the 5-year US Treasury).
    A. If a manager purchased the ABC Corporate issue and entered into a swap to pay fixed and receive floating, what spread over Libor is realized until the first swap reset date?
    B. Why would a total return manager buy the issue and then enter into a swap to pay fixed and receive floating?
15. The following was reported in the "Strategies" section of the January 3, 2000 issue of *BondWeek* ("Chicago Trust to Move Up in Credit Quality," p. 10):

> The Chicago Trust Co. plans to buy single-A corporate bonds with intermediate maturities starting this quarter, as the firm swaps out of lower-rated, triple B rated paper to take advantage of attractive spreads from an anticipated flood of single-A supply. . . .

The portfolio manager gave the following reasoning for the trade:

> ... he says a lack of single-A corporate offerings during the fourth quarter has made the paper rich, and he expects it will result in a surge of issuance by single-A rated companies this quarter, blowing out spreads and creating buying opportunities. Once the issuance subsides by the end of the quarter, he expects spreads on the single-A paper will tighten.

A. What type of relative value analysis is the portfolio manager relying on in making this swap decision and what are the underlying assumptions? (Note: When answering this question, keep the following in mind. The manager made the statement at either the last few days of December 1999 or the first two days in January 2000. So, reference to the fourth quarter means the last quarter in 1999. When the statement refers to the end of the quarter or to "this quarter" it is meant the first quarter of 2000.)

B. Further in the article, it was stated that the portfolio manager felt that on an historical basis the corporate market as a whole was cheap. The portfolio manager used new cash to purchase healthcare credits, doubling the portfolio's allocation to the healthcare sector. The portfolio manager felt that the issuers in the healthcare sector he purchased for the portfolio had fallen out of favor with investors as a result of concerns with healthcare reform. He thought that the cash flows for the issuers purchased were strong and the concerns regarding reform were "overblown." Discuss the key elements to this strategy.

16. The following was reported in the "Strategies" section of the January 3, 2000 issue of *BondWeek* (". . . Even as Wright Moves Down." p. 10):

> Wright Investors Services plans to buy triple B-rated corporate paper in the industrial sector and sell higher rated corporate paper on the view that stronger-than-anticipated economic growth will allay corporate bond investor fears.

In the article, the following was noted about the portfolio manager's view:

> spreads on higher rated investment grade paper already have come in some from last summer's wides, but he believes concerns over year-end and rising rates have kept investors from buying lower rated corporate paper, keeping spreads relatively wide.

Discuss the motivation for this strategy and the underlying assumptions.

17. The following appeared in the "Strategies" section of the September 27, 1999 issue of *BondWeek* ("Firm Sticks to Corps, Agencies," p. 6):

> The firm, which is already overweight in corporates, expects to invest cash in single A corporate paper in non-cyclical consumer non-durable sectors, which should outperform lower-quality, cyclicals as the economy begins to slow.

Discuss this strategy and its assumptions.

18. A. Suppose that a manager believes that credit spreads are mean reverting. Below are three issues along with the current spread, the mean (average) spread over the past six months, and the standard deviation of the spread. Assuming that the spreads

are normally distributed, which issue is the most likely to be purchased based on mean-reversion analysis?

Issue	Current Spread	Mean Spread for Past 6 Months	Standard Deviation of Spread
A	110 bps	85 bps	25 bps
B	124	100	10
C	130	110	15

B. What are the underlying assumptions in using mean-reversion analysis?

19. Ms. Xu is the senior portfolio manager for the Solid Income Mutual Fund. The fund invests primarily in investment-grade credit and agency mortgage-backed securities. For each quarterly meeting of the board of directors of the mutual fund, Ms. Xu provides information on the characteristics of the portfolio and changes in the composition of the portfolio since the previous board meeting. One of the board members notices two changes in the composition of the portfolio. First, he notices that while the percentage of the portfolio invested in credit was unchanged, there was a sizeable reduction in callable credit relative to noncallable credit bonds. Second, while the portfolio had the same percentage of mortgage passthrough securities, there was a greater percentage of low-coupon securities relative to high-coupon securities.

    When Ms. Xu was asked why she changed the structural characteristics of the securities in the portfolio, she responded that it was because the management team expects a significant drop in interest rates in the next quarter and the new structures would benefit more from declining interest rates than the structures held in the previous quarter. One of the directors asked why. How should Ms. Xu respond?

20. Ms. Smith is the portfolio manager of the Good Corporate Bond Fund, which invests primarily in investment-grade corporate bonds. The fund currently has an overweight within the retail industrial sector bonds of retailers. Ms. Smith is concerned that increased competition from internet retailers will negatively affect the earnings and cash flow of the traditional retailers. The fund is also currently underweighted in the US dollar-denominated bonds of European issuers placed in the United States, which she believes should benefit from increased opportunities afforded by European Union. She believes that many of these companies may come to market with new US dollar issues to fund some of their expansion throughout Europe.

    Formulate and support a strategy for Ms. Smith that will capitalize on her views about the retail and European corporate sectors of her portfolio. What factors might negatively impact this strategy?

The following information relates to Questions 21–26 and is based on "Fixed-Income Portfolio Management—Part I" and this chapter

Coughlin Fixed Income Funds is a family of mutual funds with assets totaling $4 billion, comprised primarily of US corporate bonds. Hanover-Green Life Insurance Company has just under $1 billion in total assets primarily invested in US corporate bonds. The two companies are considering combining their research and analysis units into one entity. They are also looking at possible synergies from consolidating their trading desks and/or back-office operations. Over a longer horizon, the companies also are open to the possibility of merger.

Gaven Warren is a senior portfolio manager with Hanover-Green. He has been asked to review the prospectuses for the various Coughlin funds and make recommendations regarding how the two companies might combine operations. Specifically, Warren is reviewing three of Coughlin's funds—The Select High-Performance Fund, the Yield Curve Plus Fund, and the Index Match Fund. Highlights of the investment objectives of the three funds are shown below:

> The Select High-Performance Fund relies on the superior skills of its analyst team to discover hidden values among a wide range of corporate fixed-income securities. The fund will be approximately 95 percent invested in US dollar denominated corporate bonds with medium-term to long-term maturities and Standard & Poors ratings of B or higher. The fund may use options, futures, and other derivative products to enhance returns. The primary goal of the fund is to maximize total return. The fund's annual total return target is to exceed the Lehman Brothers US Corporate Bond Index total return by 200 basis points.
>
> The Yield Curve Plus Fund uses selected investments at key points along the yield curve to enhance portfolio returns. The fund will be approximately 95 percent invested in US dollar denominated corporate bonds with medium-term to long-term maturities and Standard & Poors ratings of BBB or higher. The fund may use options, futures, and other derivative products to enhance returns. The primary goal of the fund is to outperform the Lehman Brothers US Corporate Bond Index by analyzing the yield curve appropriate to pricing corporate bonds, identifying key rate durations for the bonds held in the portfolio, and positioning the portfolio to benefit from anticipated shifts in the slope and shape of the yield curve.
>
> The Index Match Fund seeks to match the return on the Lehman Brothers US Corporate Bond Index. The fund will be approximately 98 percent invested in US dollar denominated corporate bonds with medium-term to long-term maturities and Standard & Poors ratings of BBB or higher. The fund may use options, futures, and other derivative products to match the Lehman Brothers US Corporate Bond Index returns.

As is typical of life insurance companies, Hanover-Green has estimated its liabilities using standard actuarial methods. The weighted-average duration of Hanover-Green's liabilities is about 12 years. The long-term focus of Hanover-Green means they can tolerate low liquidity in their portfolio. The primary management technique used by Hanover-Green has been contingent immunization. Because Warren anticipates a discussion with Coughlin regarding contingent immunization, he has prepared the following statements as part of a presentation.

Statement 1 "Contingent immunization requires the prevailing immunized rate of return to exceed the required rate of return."

Statement 2 "When interest rates fall, contingent immunization switches to more active management because the dollar safety margin is higher."

Although the Lehman Brothers US Corporate Bond Index is the benchmark for the Coughlin funds, Warren is not certain that the index is appropriate for Hanover-Green. He compiled the data given in Exhibit 1 as a step toward deciding what index might be the best benchmark for Hanover-Green.

EXHIBIT 1 Selected Characteristics, Bond Indexes

Index	Effective Duration	YTM (%)	Average Coupon (%)	Number of Securities	Weighting
Long-Term US Corporate Bond Index	8.65	5.75	5.25	558	Value
Global Government Bond Index	5.15	6.30	5.85	520	Value
Selected Municipal Bonds Index	4.65	4.87	4.75	20	Value
Equal-Weighted Corporate Bond Index	4.70	5.19	5.75	96	Equal

Hanover-Green is considering a more active style for a small part of its portfolio. Warren is investigating several relative value methodologies. Two approaches are of particular interest—primary market analysis and spread analysis. Warren is worried that the primary market is about to enter a period where the supply of new issues will increase causing spreads to tighten, and furthermore, that most of the new issues will not be callable.

Regarding spread analysis, Hanover-Green is considering the addition of mortgage-backed securities (MBS) to its portfolio. Warren has investigated the MBS market and found that MBS analysis emphasizes the option-adjusted spread (OAS). Warren is considering using OAS to measure the risk of the corporate bonds in Hanover-Green's portfolio. Specifically, he wants to analyze the risks involved in holding several bonds whose credit ratings have deteriorated to speculative status.

21. The strategy used by the Yield Curve Plus Fund *most likely* attempts to enhance portfolio returns by taking advantage of:
    A. changes in credit spreads.
    B. changes in the level of interest rates.
    C. nonparallel changes in the yield curve.
22. The contingent immunization technique that Hanover-Green currently uses in managing their fixed-income portfolio is *best* described as:
    A. a passive management strategy similar to that of the Index Match Fund.
    B. an active management strategy similar to that of the Select High-Performance Fund.
    C. a mix of active and passive management strategies similar to that of the Yield Curve Plus Fund.
23. Are Warren's statements regarding contingent immunization *most likely* correct or incorrect?

	Statement 1	Statement 2
A.	Correct	Correct
B.	Correct	Incorrect
C.	Incorrect	Correct

24. Based solely on the information in Exhibit 1, which index is the *most* appropriate benchmark for Hanover-Green's portfolio?
    A. Global Government Bond Index.
    B. Long-Term US Corporate Bond Index.
    C. Equal-Weighted Corporate Bond Index.

25. Consider Warren's expectations regarding the supply of new issues in the primary market. Given recent research into primary markets, is Warren ***most likely*** correct or incorrect regarding the effect on spreads and the probability of the bonds being callable?

	Effect on Spreads	Bonds Being Callable
A.	Correct	Correct
B.	Correct	Incorrect
C.	Incorrect	Correct

26. Which of the following statements ***most*** accurately evaluates the use of the option-adjusted spread (OAS) to analyze the bonds held in Hanover-Green's portfolio?
    A. OAS excludes default risk from its calculation; therefore OAS has limited applicability to the analysis of speculative grade bonds.
    B. OAS uses Monte Carlo simulation to factor out default risk from the spread; therefore OAS is not well suited to the analysis of speculative grade bonds.
    C. OAS is often used to evaluate bonds other than mortgage-backed securities. It is a very useful tool, especially appropriate for high-risk positions such as speculative grade bonds.

PART II

SOLUTIONS

CHAPTER 1

FIXED-INCOME SECURITIES: DEFINING ELEMENTS

SOLUTIONS

1. A is correct. The tenor of the bond is the time remaining until the bond's maturity date. Although the bond had a maturity of 10 years at issuance (original maturity), it was issued four years ago. Thus, there are six years remaining until the maturity date.

   B is incorrect because the nominal rate is the coupon rate—that is, the interest rate that the issuer agrees to pay each year until the maturity date. Although interest is paid semi-annually, the nominal rate is 10%, not 5%. C is incorrect because it is the bond's price, not its redemption value (also called principal amount, principal value, par value, face value, nominal value, or maturity value), that is equal to 102% of the par value.
2. C is correct. A capital market security has an original maturity longer than one year.

   A is incorrect because a perpetual bond does not have a stated maturity date. Thus, the sovereign bond, which has a maturity of 15 years, cannot be a perpetual bond. B is incorrect because a pure discount bond is a bond issued at a discount to par value and redeemed at par. Some sovereign bonds (e.g., Treasury bills) are pure discount bonds, but others are not.
3. C is correct. The coupon rate that applies to the interest payment due on 30 June is based on the three-month Libor rate prevailing on 31 March. Thus, the coupon rate is 1.55% + 0.65% = 2.20%.
4. B is correct. The indenture, also referred to as trust deed, is the legal contract that describes the form of the bond, the obligations of the issuer, and the rights of the bondholders.

   A is incorrect because covenants are only one element of a bond's indenture. Covenants are clauses that specify the rights of the bondholders and any actions that the issuer is obligated to perform or prohibited from performing. C is incorrect because a debenture is a type of bond. In many jurisdictions, debentures are unsecured bonds.
5. B is correct. A surety bond is an external credit enhancement, that is, a guarantee received from a third party. If the issuer defaults, the guarantor who provided the surety

bond will reimburse investors for any losses, usually up to a maximum amount called the penal sum.

A is incorrect because covenants are legally enforceable rules that borrowers and lenders agree upon when the bond is issued. C is incorrect because overcollateralization is an internal, not external, credit enhancement. Collateral is a guarantee underlying the debt above and beyond the issuer's promise to pay, and overcollateralization refers to the process of posting more collateral than is needed to obtain or secure financing. Collateral, such as assets or securities pledged to ensure debt payments, is not provided by a third party. Thus, overcollateralization is not an external credit enhancement.

6. B is correct. Affirmative (or positive) covenants enumerate what issuers are required to do and are typically administrative in nature. A common affirmative covenant describes what the issuer intends to do with the proceeds from the bond issue.

   A and C are incorrect because imposing a limit on the issuer's leverage ratio or on the percentage of the issuer's gross assets that can be sold are negative covenants. Negative covenants prevent the issuer from taking actions that could reduce its ability to make interest payments and repay the principal.

7. B is correct. Prohibiting the issuer from investing in risky projects restricts the issuer's potential business decisions. These restrictions are referred to as negative bond covenants.

   A and C are incorrect because paying taxes as they come due and maintaining the current lines of business are positive covenants.

8. C is correct. Bonds sold in a country and denominated in that country's currency by an entity from another country are referred to as foreign bonds.

   A is incorrect because Eurobonds are bonds issued outside the jurisdiction of any single country. B is incorrect because global bonds are bonds issued in the Eurobond market and at least one domestic country simultaneously.

9. A is correct. Eurobonds are typically issued as bearer bonds, that is, bonds for which the trustee does not keep records of ownership. In contrast, domestic and foreign bonds are typically registered bonds for which ownership is recorded by either name or serial number.

   B is incorrect because Eurobonds are typically issued as bearer bonds, not registered bonds. C is incorrect because Eurobonds are typically subject to lower, not greater, regulation than domestic and foreign bonds.

10. C is correct. The original issue discount tax provision requires the investor to include a prorated portion of the original issue discount in his taxable income every tax year until maturity. The original issue discount is equal to the difference between the bond's par value and its original issue price.

    A is incorrect because the original issue discount tax provision allows the investor to increase his cost basis in the bond so that when the bond matures, he faces no capital gain or loss. B is incorrect because the original issue discount tax provision does not require any tax deduction in the year the bond is purchased or afterward.

11. C is correct. A fully amortized bond calls for equal cash payments by the bond's issuer prior to maturity. Each fixed payment includes both an interest payment component and a principal repayment component such that the bond's outstanding principal amount is reduced to zero by the maturity date.

    A and B are incorrect because a bullet bond or plain vanilla bond only make interest payments prior to maturity. The entire principal repayment occurs at maturity.

12. C is correct. A cap in a floating-rate note (capped FRN) prevents the coupon rate from increasing above a specified maximum rate. This feature benefits the issuer in a rising interest rate environment because it sets a limit to the interest rate paid on the debt.

A is incorrect because a bond with a step-up coupon is one in which the coupon, which may be fixed or floating, increases by specified margins at specified dates. This feature benefits the bondholders, not the issuer, in a rising interest rate environment because it allows bondholders to receive a higher coupon in line with the higher market interest rates. B is incorrect because inflation-linked bonds have their coupon payments and/or principal repayment linked to an index of consumer prices. If interest rates increase as a result of inflation, this feature is a benefit for the bondholders, not the issuer.

13. C is correct. In contrast to fixed-rate bonds that decline in value in a rising interest rate environment, floating-rate notes (FRNs) are less affected when interest rates increase because their coupon rates vary with market interest rates and are reset at regular, short-term intervals. Consequently, FRNs are favored by investors who believe that interest rates will rise.

    A is incorrect because an inverse floater is a bond whose coupon rate has an inverse relationship to the reference rate, so when interest rates rise, the coupon rate on an inverse floater decreases. Thus, inverse floaters are favored by investors who believe that interest rates will decline, not rise. B is incorrect because fixed rate-bonds decline in value in a rising interest rate environment. Consequently, investors who expect interest rates to rise will likely avoid investing in fixed-rate bonds.
14. C is correct. Capital-indexed bonds pay a fixed coupon rate that is applied to a principal amount that increases in line with increases in the index during the bond's life. If the consumer price index increases by 2%, the coupon rate remains unchanged at 6%, but the principal amount increases by 2% and the coupon payment is based on the inflation-adjusted principal amount. On the first coupon payment date, the inflation-adjusted principal amount is $1{,}000 \times (1 + 0.02) = 1{,}020$ and the semi-annual coupon payment is equal to $(0.06 \times 1{,}020) \div 2 = 30.60$.
15. A is correct. A put provision provides bondholders the right to sell the bond back to the issuer at a predetermined price prior to the bond's maturity date.

    B is incorrect because a make-whole call provision is a form of call provision; that is, a provision that provides the issuer the right to redeem all or part of the bond before its maturity date. A make-whole call provision requires the issuer to make a lump sum payment to the bondholders based on the present value of the future coupon payments and principal repayments not paid because of the bond being redeemed early by the issuer. C is incorrect because an original issue discount provision is a tax provision relating to bonds issued at a discount to par value. The original issue discount tax provision typically requires the bondholders to include a prorated portion of the original issue discount (i.e., the difference between the par value and the original issue price) in their taxable income every tax year until the bond's maturity date.
16. B is correct. A call provision (callable bond) gives the issuer the right to redeem all or part of the bond before the specified maturity date. If market interest rates decline or the issuer's credit quality improves, the issuer of a callable bond can redeem it and replace it by a cheaper bond. Thus, the call provision is beneficial to the issuer.

    A is incorrect because a put provision (putable bond) is beneficial to the bondholders. If interest rates rise, thus lowering the bond's price, the bondholders have the right to sell the bond back to the issuer at a predetermined price on specified dates. C is incorrect because a conversion provision (convertible bond) is beneficial to the bondholders. If the issuing company's share price increases, the bondholders have the right to exchange the bond for a specified number of common shares in the issuing company.

17. A is correct. A put feature is beneficial to the bondholders. Thus, the price of a putable bond will typically be higher than the price of an otherwise similar non-putable bond.

    B is incorrect because a call feature is beneficial to the issuer. Thus, the price of a callable bond will typically be lower, not higher, than the price of an otherwise similar non-callable bond. C is incorrect because a conversion feature is beneficial to the bondholders. Thus, the price of a convertible bond will typically be higher, not lower, than the price of an otherwise similar non-convertible bond.

CHAPTER 2

FIXED-INCOME MARKETS: ISSUANCE, TRADING, AND FUNDING

SOLUTIONS

1. C is correct. In most countries, the largest issuers of bonds are the national and local governments as well as financial institutions. Thus, the bond market sector with the smallest amount of bonds outstanding is the non-financial corporate sector.
2. B is correct. The distinction between investment grade and non-investment grade debt relates to differences in credit quality, not tax status or maturity dates. Debt markets are classified based on the issuer's creditworthiness as judged by the credit ratings agencies. Ratings of Baa3 or above by Moody's Investors Service or BBB– or above by Standard & Poor's and Fitch Ratings are considered investment grade, whereas ratings below these levels are referred to as non-investment grade (also called high yield, speculative, or junk).
3. A is correct. Eurobonds are issued internationally, outside the jurisdiction of any single country. B is incorrect because foreign bonds are considered international bonds, but they are issued in a specific country, in the currency of that country, by an issuer domiciled in another country. C is incorrect because municipal bonds are US domestic bonds issued by a state or local government.
4. B is correct. Many emerging countries lag developed countries in the areas of political stability, property rights, and contract enforcement. Consequently, emerging market bonds usually exhibit higher risk than developed markets bonds. A is incorrect because emerging markets bonds typically offer higher (not lower) yields than developed markets bonds to compensate investors for the higher risk. C is incorrect because emerging markets bonds usually benefit from higher (not lower) growth prospects than developed markets bonds.
5. B is correct. The coupon rate of a floating-rate bond is expressed as a reference rate plus a spread. Different reference rates are used depending on where the bond is issued and its

currency denomination, but one of the most widely used set of reference rates is Libor. A and C are incorrect because a bond's spread and frequency of coupon payments are typically set when the bond is issued and do not change during the bond's life.

6. C is correct. Interbank offered rates are used as reference rates not only for floating-rate bonds, but also for other debt instruments including mortgages, derivatives such as interest rate and currency swaps, and many other financial contracts and products. A and B are incorrect because an interbank offered rate such as Libor or Euribor is a set of reference rates (not a single reference rate) for different borrowing periods of up to one year (not 10 years).
7. A is correct. In an underwritten offering (also called firm commitment offering), the investment bank (called the underwriter) guarantees the sale of the bond issue at an offering price that is negotiated with the issuer. Thus, the underwriter takes the risk of buying the newly issued bonds from the issuer, and then reselling them to investors or to dealers who then sell them to investors. B and C are incorrect because the bond issuing mechanism where an investment bank acts as a broker and receives a commission for selling the bonds to investors, and incurs less risk associated with selling the bonds, is a best efforts offering (not an underwritten offering).
8. A is correct. In major developed bond markets, newly issued sovereign bonds are sold to the public via an auction. B and C are incorrect because sovereign bonds are rarely issued via private placements or best effort offerings.
9. B is correct. A shelf registration allows certain authorized issuers to offer additional bonds to the general public without having to prepare a new and separate offering circular. The issuer can offer multiple bond issuances under the same master prospectus, and only has to prepare a short document when additional bonds are issued. A is incorrect because the grey market is a forward market for bonds about to be issued. C is incorrect because a private placement is a non-underwritten, unregistered offering of bonds that are not sold to the general public but directly to an investor or a small group of investors.
10. B is correct. Secondary bond markets are where bonds are traded between investors. A is incorrect because newly issued bonds (whether from corporate issuers or other types of issuers) are issued in primary (not secondary) bond markets. C is incorrect because the major participants in secondary bond markets globally are large institutional investors and central banks (not retail investors).
11. C is correct. In over-the-counter (OTC) markets, buy and sell orders are initiated from various locations and then matched through a communications network. Most bonds are traded in OTC markets. A is incorrect because on organized exchanges, buy and sell orders may come from anywhere, but the transactions must take place at the exchange according to the rules imposed by the exchange. B is incorrect because open market operations refer to central bank activities in secondary bond markets. Central banks buy and sell bonds, usually sovereign bonds issued by the national government, as a means to implement monetary policy.
12. C is correct. Liquidity in secondary bond markets refers to the ability to buy or sell bonds quickly at prices close to their fair market value. A and B are incorrect because a liquid secondary bond market does not guarantee that a bond will sell at the price sought by the investor, or that the investor will not face a loss on his or her investment.
13. C is correct. Sovereign bonds are usually unsecured obligations of the national government issuing the bonds; they are not backed by collateral, but by the taxing authority of the national government. A is incorrect because bonds issued by local governments are non-sovereign (not sovereign) bonds. B is incorrect because sovereign bonds are typically unsecured (not secured) obligations of a national government.

14. C is correct. Agency bonds are issued by quasi-government entities. These entities are agencies and organizations usually established by national governments to perform various functions for them. A and B are incorrect because local and national governments issue non-sovereign and sovereign bonds, respectively.
15. B is correct. The IMF is a multilateral agency that issues supranational bonds. A and C are incorrect because sovereign bonds and quasi-government bonds are issued by national governments and by entities that perform various functions for national governments, respectively.
16. C is correct. Companies use commercial paper not only as a source of funding working capital and seasonal demand for cash, but also as a source of interim financing for long-term projects until permanent financing can be arranged. A is incorrect because there is a secondary market for trading commercial paper, although trading is limited except for the largest issues. B is incorrect because commercial paper is issued by companies across the risk spectrum, although only the strongest, highly rated companies issue *low-cost* commercial paper.
17. A is correct. Commercial paper, whether US commercial paper or Eurocommercial paper, is negotiable—that is, investors can buy and sell commercial paper on secondary markets. B is incorrect because Eurocommercial paper can be denominated in any currency. C is incorrect because Eurocommercial paper is more frequently issued on an interest-bearing (or yield) basis than on a discount basis.
18. A is correct. A sinking fund arrangement is a way to reduce credit risk by making the issuer set aside funds over time to retire the bond issue. B and C are incorrect because a sinking fund arrangement has no effect on inflation risk or interest rate risk.
19. C is correct. Wholesale funds available for banks include central bank funds, interbank funds, and negotiable certificates of deposit. A and B are incorrect because demand deposits (also known as checking accounts) and money market accounts are retail deposits (not wholesale funds).
20. B is correct. A negotiable certificate of deposit (CD) allows any depositor (initial or subsequent) to sell the CD in the open market prior to maturity. A is incorrect because negotiable CDs are mostly available in large (not small) denominations. Large-denomination negotiable CDs are an important source of wholesale funds for banks, whereas small-denomination CDs are not. C is incorrect because a penalty is imposed if the depositor withdraws funds prior to maturity for non-negotiable (instead of negotiable) CDs.
21. B is correct. A repurchase agreement (repo) can be viewed as a collateralized loan where the security sold and subsequently repurchased represents the collateral posted. A and C are incorrect because interbank deposits and negotiable certificates of deposit are unsecured deposits—that is, there is no collateral backing the deposit.
22. A is correct. The repo margin (the difference between the market value of the underlying collateral and the value of the loan) is a function of the supply and demand conditions of the collateral. The repo margin is typically lower if the underlying collateral is in short supply or if there is a high demand for it. B and C are incorrect because the repo margin is usually higher (not lower) when the maturity of the repurchase agreement is long and when the credit risk associated with the underlying collateral is high.

CHAPTER 3

INTRODUCTION TO FIXED-INCOME VALUATION

SOLUTIONS

1. B is correct. The bond price is closest to 101.36. The price is determined in the following manner:

$$PV = \frac{PMT}{(1+r)^1} + \frac{PMT}{(1+r)^2} + \frac{PMT + FV}{(1+r)^3}$$

where:

PV = present value, or the price of the bond
PMT = coupon payment per period
FV = future value paid at maturity, or the par value of the bond
r = market discount rate, or required rate of return per period

$$PV = \frac{5.5}{(1+0.05)^1} + \frac{5.5}{(1+0.05)^2} + \frac{5.5 + 100}{(1+0.05)^3}$$

$$PV = 5.24 + 4.99 + 91.13 = 101.36$$

2. C is correct. The bond price is closest to 98.11. The formula for calculating the price of this bond is:

$$PV = \frac{PMT}{(1+r)^1} + \frac{PMT + FV}{(1+r)^2}$$

where:

PV = present value, or the price of the bond
PMT = coupon payment per period
FV = future value paid at maturity, or the par value of the bond
r = market discount rate, or required rate of return per period

$$PV = \frac{3}{(1+0.04)^1} + \frac{3+100}{(1+0.04)^2} = 2.88 + 95.23 = 98.11$$

3. A is correct. The bond price is closest to 95.00. The bond has six semiannual periods. Half of the annual coupon is paid in each period with the required rate of return also being halved. The price is determined in the following manner:

$$PV = \frac{PMT}{(1+r)^1} + \frac{PMT}{(1+r)^2} + \frac{PMT}{(1+r)^3} + \frac{PMT}{(1+r)^4} + \frac{PMT}{(1+r)^5} + \frac{PMT+FV}{(1+r)^6}$$

where:

PV = present value, or the price of the bond
PMT = coupon payment per period
FV = future value paid at maturity, or the par value of the bond
r = market discount rate, or required rate of return per period

$$PV = \frac{4.5}{(1+0.055)^1} + \frac{4.5}{(1+0.055)^2} + \frac{4.5}{(1+0.055)^3} + \frac{4.5}{(1+0.055)^4} + \frac{4.5}{(1+0.055)^5} + \frac{4.5+100}{(1+0.055)^6}$$

$PV = 4.27 + 4.04 + 3.83 + 3.63 + 3.44 + 75.79 = 95.00$

4. B is correct. The bond price is closest to 96.28. The formula for calculating this bond price is:

$$PV = \frac{PMT}{(1+r)^1} + \frac{PMT}{(1+r)^2} + \frac{PMT}{(1+r)^3} + \frac{PMT+FV}{(1+r)^4}$$

where:

PV = present value, or the price of the bond
PMT = coupon payment per period
FV = future value paid at maturity, or the par value of the bond
r = market discount rate, or required rate of return per period

$$PV = \frac{2}{(1+0.03)^1} + \frac{2}{(1+0.03)^2} + \frac{2}{(1+0.03)^3} + \frac{2+100}{(1+0.03)^4}$$

$PV = 1.94 + 1.89 + 1.83 + 90.62 = 96.28$

5. B is correct. The bond price is closest to 112.54. The formula for calculating this bond price is:

$$PV = \frac{PMT}{(1+r)^1} + \frac{PMT}{(1+r)^2} + \frac{PMT}{(1+r)^3} + \cdots + \frac{PMT+FV}{(1+r)^{14}}$$

where:

PV = present value, or the price of the bond
PMT = coupon payment per period
FV = future value paid at maturity, or the par value of the bond
r = market discount rate, or required rate of return per period

$$PV = \frac{2.5}{(1+0.015)^1} + \frac{2.5}{(1+0.015)^2} + \frac{2.5}{(1+0.015)^3} + \cdots + \frac{2.5}{(1+0.015)^{13}} + \frac{2.5+100}{(1+0.015)^{14}}$$

$$PV = 2.46 + 2.43 + 2.39 + \cdots + 2.06 + 83.21 = 112.54$$

6. B is correct. The price of the zero-coupon bond is closest to 51.67. The price is determined in the following manner:

$$PV = \frac{100}{(1+r)^N}$$

where:

PV = present value, or the price of the bond
r = market discount rate, or required rate of return per period
N = number of evenly spaced periods to maturity

$$PV = \frac{100}{(1+0.045)^{15}}$$

$$PV = 51.67$$

7. B is correct. The price difference between Bonds A and B is closest to 3.77. One method for calculating the price difference between two bonds with an identical term to maturity is to use the following formula:

$$PV = \frac{PMT}{(1+r)^1} + \frac{PMT}{(1+r)^2}$$

where:

PV = price difference
PMT = coupon difference per period
r = market discount rate, or required rate of return per period

In this case the coupon difference is (5% – 3%), or 2%.

$$PV = \frac{2}{(1+0.04)^1} + \frac{2}{(1+0.04)^2} = 1.92 + 1.85 = 3.77$$

8. A is correct. Bond A offers the lowest yield-to-maturity. When a bond is priced at a premium above par value the yield-to-maturity (YTM), or market discount rate is less than the coupon rate. Bond A is priced at a premium, so its YTM is below its 5% coupon rate. Bond B is priced at par value so its YTM is equal to its 6% coupon rate. Bond C is priced at a discount below par value, so its YTM is above its 5% coupon rate.
9. B is correct. Bond B will most likely experience the smallest percent change in price if market discount rates increase by 100 basis points (bps). A higher-coupon bond has a smaller percentage price change than a lower-coupon bond when their market discount rates change by the same amount (the coupon effect). Also, a shorter-term bond generally has a smaller percentage price change than a longer-term bond when their market discount rates change by the same amount (the maturity effect). Bond B will experience a smaller percent change in price than Bond A because of the coupon effect. Bond B will also experience a smaller percent change in price than Bond C because of the coupon effect and the maturity effect.

10. B is correct. The bond price is most likely to change by less than 5%. The relationship between bond prices and market discount rate is not linear. The percentage price change is greater in absolute value when the market discount rate goes down than when it goes up by the same amount (the convexity effect). If a 100 basis point decrease in the market discount rate will cause the price of the bond to increase by 5%, then a 100 basis point increase in the market discount rate will cause the price of the bond to decline by an amount less than 5%.
11. B is correct. Generally, for two bonds with the same time-to-maturity, a lower coupon bond will experience a greater percentage price change than a higher coupon bond when their market discount rates change by the same amount. Bond B and Bond C have the same time-to-maturity (5 years); however, Bond B offers a lower coupon rate. Therefore, Bond B will likely experience a greater percentage change in price in comparison to Bond C.
12. A is correct. Bond A will likely experience the greatest percent change in price due to the coupon effect and the maturity effect. For two bonds with the same time-to-maturity, a lower-coupon bond has a greater percentage price change than a higher-coupon bond when their market discount rates change by the same amount. Generally, for the same coupon rate, a longer-term bond has a greater percentage price change than a shorter-term bond when their market discount rates change by the same amount. Relative to Bond C, Bond A and Bond B both offer the same lower coupon rate of 6%; however, Bond A has a longer time-to-maturity than Bond B. Therefore, Bond A will likely experience the greater percentage change in price if the market discount rates for all three bonds increase by 100 bps.
13. A is correct. The bond price is closest to 101.93. The price is determined in the following manner:

$$PV = \frac{PMT}{(1+Z_1)^1} + \frac{PMT + FV}{(1+Z_2)^2}$$

where:

PV = present value, or the price of the bond
PMT = coupon payment per period
FV = future value paid at maturity, or the par value of the bond
Z_1 = spot rate, or the zero-coupon yield, for Period 1
Z_2 = spot rate, or the zero-coupon yield, for Period 2

$$PV = \frac{5}{(1+0.03)^1} + \frac{5+100}{(1+0.04)^2}$$

$$PV = 4.85 + 97.08 = 101.93$$

14. B is correct. The bond price is closest to 101.46. The price is determined in the following manner:

$$PV = \frac{PMT}{(1+Z_1)^1} + \frac{PMT}{(1+Z_2)^2} + \frac{PMT + FV}{(1+Z_3)^3}$$

where:

PV = present value, or the price of the bond
PMT = coupon payment per period
FV = future value paid at maturity, or the par value of the bond
Z_1 = spot rate, or the zero-coupon yield, or zero rate, for period 1
Z_2 = spot rate, or the zero-coupon yield, or zero rate, for period 2
Z_3 = spot rate, or the zero-coupon yield, or zero rate, for period 3

$$PV = \frac{10}{(1+0.08)^1} + \frac{10}{(1+0.09)^2} + \frac{10+100}{(1+0.095)^3}$$

$$PV = 9.26 + 8.42 + 83.78 = 101.46$$

15. B is correct. The bond price is closest to 95.28. The formula for calculating this bond price is:

$$PV = \frac{PMT}{(1+Z_1)^1} + \frac{PMT}{(1+Z_2)^2} + \frac{PMT+FV}{(1+Z_3)^3}$$

where:

PV = present value, or the price of the bond
PMT = coupon payment per period
FV = future value paid at maturity, or the par value of the bond
Z_1 = spot rate, or the zero-coupon yield, or zero rate, for period 1
Z_2 = spot rate, or the zero-coupon yield, or zero rate, for period 2
Z_3 = spot rate, or the zero-coupon yield, or zero rate, for period 3

$$PV = \frac{8}{(1+0.08)^1} + \frac{8}{(1+0.09)^2} + \frac{8+100}{(1+0.10)^3}$$

$$PV = 7.41 + 6.73 + 81.14 = 95.28$$

16. C is correct. The bond price is closest to 92.76. The formula for calculating this bond price is:

$$PV = \frac{PMT}{(1+Z_1)^1} + \frac{PMT}{(1+Z_2)^2} + \frac{PMT+FV}{(1+Z_3)^3}$$

where:

PV = present value, or the price of the bond
PMT = coupon payment per period
FV = future value paid at maturity, or the par value of the bond
Z_1 = spot rate, or the zero-coupon yield, or zero rate, for period 1
Z_2 = spot rate, or the zero-coupon yield, or zero rate, for period 2
Z_3 = spot rate, or the zero-coupon yield, or zero rate, for period 3

$$PV = \frac{7}{(1+0.08)^1} + \frac{7}{(1+0.09)^2} + \frac{7+100}{(1+0.10)^3}$$

$$PV = 6.48 + 5.89 + 80.39 = 92.76$$

17. B is correct. The yield-to-maturity is closest to 9.92%. The formula for calculating the price of Bond Z is:

$$PV = \frac{PMT}{(1+Z_1)^1} + \frac{PMT}{(1+Z_2)^2} + \frac{PMT+FV}{(1+Z_3)^3}$$

where:

PV = present value, or the price of the bond
PMT = coupon payment per period
FV = future value paid at maturity, or the par value of the bond
Z_1 = spot rate, or the zero-coupon yield, or zero rate, for period 1
Z_2 = spot rate, or the zero-coupon yield, or zero rate, for period 2
Z_3 = spot rate, or the zero-coupon yield, or zero rate, for period 3

$$PV = \frac{6}{(1+0.08)^1} + \frac{6}{(1+0.09)^2} + \frac{6+100}{(1+0.10)^3}$$

$$PV = 5.56 + 5.05 + 79.64 = 90.25$$

Using this price, the bond's yield-to-maturity can be calculated as:

$$PV = \frac{PMT}{(1+r)^1} + \frac{PMT}{(1+r)^2} + \frac{PMT+FV}{(1+r)^3}$$

$$90.25 = \frac{6}{(1+r)^1} + \frac{6}{(1+r)^2} + \frac{6+100}{(1+r)^3}$$

$$r = 9.92\%$$

18. A is correct. Bond dealers usually quote the flat price. When a trade takes place, the accrued interest is added to the flat price to obtain the full price paid by the buyer and received by the seller on the settlement date. The reason for using the flat price for quotation is to avoid misleading investors about the market price trend for the bond. If the full price were to be quoted by dealers, investors would see the price rise day after day even if the yield-to-maturity did not change. That is because the amount of accrued interest increases each day. Then after the coupon payment is made the quoted price would drop dramatically. Using the flat price for quotation avoids that misrepresentation. The full price, flat price plus accrued interest, is not usually quoted by bond dealers. Accrued interest is included in, not added to, the full price, and bond dealers do not generally quote the full price.

19. B is correct. The bond's full price is 103.10. The price is determined in the following manner:

As of the beginning of the coupon period on 10 April 2014, there are 2.5 years (5 semiannual periods) to maturity. These five semiannual periods occur on 10 October 2014, 10 April 2015, 10 October 2015, 10 April 2016, and 10 October 2016.

$$PV = \frac{PMT}{(1+r)^1} + \frac{PMT}{(1+r)^2} + \frac{PMT}{(1+r)^3} + \frac{PMT}{(1+r)^4} + \frac{PMT+FV}{(1+r)^5}$$

where:

PV = present value
PMT = coupon payment per period
FV = future value paid at maturity, or the par value of the bond
r = market discount rate, or required rate of return per period

$$PV = \frac{2.5}{(1+0.02)^1} + \frac{2.5}{(1+0.02)^2} + \frac{2.5}{(1+0.02)^3} + \frac{2.5}{(1+0.02)^4} + \frac{2.5+100}{(1+0.02)^5}$$

$$PV = 2.45 + 2.40 + 2.36 + 2.31 + 92.84 = 102.36$$

The accrued interest period is identified as 66/180. The number of days between 10 April 2014 and 16 June 2014 is 66 days based on the 30/360 day-count convention. (This is 20 days remaining in April + 30 days in May + 16 days in June = 66 days total). The number of days between coupon periods is assumed to be 180 days using the 30/360 day convention.

$$PV^{Full} = PV \times (1+r)^{66/180}$$

$$PV^{Full} = 102.36 \times (1.02)^{66/180} = 103.10$$

20. C is correct. The accrued interest per 100 of par value is closest to 0.92. The accrued interest is determined in the following manner: The accrued interest period is identified as 66/180. The number of days between 10 April 2014 and 16 June 2014 is 66 days based on the 30/360 day-count convention. (This is 20 days remaining in April + 30 days in May + 16 days in June = 66 days total). The number of days between coupon periods is assumed to be 180 days using the 30/360 day convention.

$$\text{Accrued interest} = \frac{t}{T} \times PMT$$

where:

t = number of days from the last coupon payment to the settlement date
T = number of days in the coupon period
t/T = fraction of the coupon period that has gone by since the last payment
PMT = coupon payment per period

$$\text{Accrued interest} = \frac{66}{180} \times \frac{5.00}{2} = 0.92$$

21. A is correct. The flat price of 102.18 is determined by subtracting the accrued interest (from question 20) from the full price (from question 19).

$$PV^{Flat} = PV^{Full} - \text{Accrued Interest}$$
$$PV^{Flat} = 103.10 - 0.92 = 102.18$$

22. B is correct. For bonds not actively traded or not yet issued, matrix pricing is a price estimation process that uses market discount rates based on the quoted prices of similar bonds (similar times-to-maturity, coupon rates, and credit quality).

23. A is correct. Matrix pricing is used in underwriting new bonds to get an estimate of the required yield spread over the benchmark rate. The benchmark rate is typically the yield-to-maturity

on a government bond having the same, or close to the same, time-to-maturity. The spread is the difference between the yield-to-maturity on the new bond and the benchmark rate. The yield spread is the additional compensation required by investors for the difference in the credit risk, liquidity risk, and tax status of the bond relative to the government bond.

In matrix pricing, the market discount rates of comparable bonds and the yield-to-maturity on a government bond having a similar time-to-maturity are not estimated. Rather they are known and used to estimate the required yield spread of a new bond.

24. B is correct. The formula for calculating this bond's yield-to-maturity is:

$$PV = \frac{PMT}{(1+r)^1} + \frac{PMT}{(1+r)^2} + \frac{PMT}{(1+r)^3} + \cdots + \frac{PMT}{(1+r)^{39}} + \frac{PMT + FV}{(1+r)^{40}}$$

where:

PV = present value, or the price of the bond
PMT = coupon payment per period
FV = future value paid at maturity, or the par value of the bond
r = market discount rate, or required rate of return per period

$$111 = \frac{2.5}{(1+r)^1} + \frac{2.5}{(1+r)^2} + \frac{2.5}{(1+r)^3} + \cdots + \frac{2.5}{(1+r)^{39}} + \frac{2.5 + 100}{(1+r)^{40}}$$

$$r = 0.0209$$

To arrive at the annualized yield-to-maturity, the semiannual rate of 2.09% must be multiplied by two. Therefore, the yield-to-maturity is equal to 2.09% × 2 = 4.18%.

25. B is correct. The annual yield-to-maturity, stated for a periodicity of 12, is 7.21%. It is calculated as follows:

$$PV = \frac{FV}{(1+r)^N}$$

$$75 = \left(\frac{100}{(1+r)^{4\times 12}}\right)$$

$$\frac{100}{75} = (1+r)^{48}$$

$$1.33333 = (1+r)^{48}$$

$$[1.33333]^{1/48} = [(1+r)^{48}]^{1/48}$$

$$1.33333^{02083} = (1+r)$$

$$1.00601 = (1+r)$$

$$1.00601 - 1 = r$$

$$0.00601 = r$$

$$r \times 12 = 0.07212, \text{ or approximately } 7.21\%$$

26. A is correct. The yield-to-maturity, stated for a periodicity of 12 (monthly periodicity), is 3.87%. The formula to convert an annual percentage rate (annual yield-to-maturity) from one periodicity to another is as follows:

$$\left(1+\frac{APR_m}{m}\right)^m = \left(1+\frac{APR_n}{n}\right)^n$$

$$\left(1+\frac{0.03897}{2}\right)^2 = \left(1+\frac{APR_{12}}{12}\right)^{12}$$

$$(1.01949)^2 = \left(1+\frac{APR_{12}}{12}\right)^{12}$$

$$1.03935 = \left(1+\frac{APR_{12}}{12}\right)^{12}$$

$$(1.03935)^{1/12} = \left[\left(1+\frac{APR_{12}}{12}\right)^{12}\right]^{1/12}$$

$$1.00322 = \left(1+\frac{APR_{12}}{12}\right)$$

$$1.00322 - 1 = \left(\frac{APR_{12}}{12}\right)$$

$APR_{12} = 0.00322 \times 12 = 0.03865$, or approximately 3.87%.

27. B is correct. The yield-to-maturity is 5.77%. The formula for calculating this bond's yield-to-maturity is:

$$PV = \frac{PMT}{(1+r)^1} + \frac{PMT}{(1+r)^2} + \frac{PMT}{(1+r)^3} + \cdots + \frac{PMT}{(1+r)^9} + \frac{PMT + FV}{(1+r)^{10}}$$

where:

PV = present value, or the price of the bond
PMT = coupon payment per period
FV = future value paid at maturity, or the par value of the bond
r = market discount rate, or required rate of return per period

$$101 = \frac{3}{(1+r)^1} + \frac{3}{(1+r)^2} + \frac{3}{(1+r)^3} + \cdots + \frac{3}{(1+r)^9} + \frac{3+100}{(1+r)^{10}}$$

$r = 0.02883$

To arrive at the annualized yield-to-maturity, the semiannual rate of 2.883% must be multiplied by two. Therefore, the yield-to-maturity is equal to 2.883% × 2 = 5.77% (rounded).

28. C is correct. The yield-to-first-call is 6.25%. Given the first call date is exactly three years away, the formula for calculating this bond's yield-to-first-call is:

$$PV = \frac{PMT}{(1+r)^1} + \frac{PMT}{(1+r)^2} + \frac{PMT}{(1+r)^3} + \cdots + \frac{PMT}{(1+r)^5} + \frac{PMT + FV}{(1+r)^6}$$

where:

PV = present value, or the price of the bond
PMT = coupon payment per period
FV = call price paid at call date
r = market discount rate, or required rate of return per period

$$101 = \frac{3}{(1+r)^1} + \frac{3}{(1+r)^2} + \frac{3}{(1+r)^3} + \cdots + \frac{3}{(1+r)^5} + \frac{3+102}{(1+r)^6}$$

$r = 0.03123$

To arrive at the annualized yield-to-first-call, the semiannual rate of 3.123% must be multiplied by two. Therefore, the yield-to-first-call is equal to 3.123% × 2 = 6.25% (rounded).

29. C is correct. The yield-to-second-call is 5.94%. Given the second call date is exactly four years away, the formula for calculating this bond's yield-to-second-call is:

$$PV = \frac{PMT}{(1+r)^1} + \frac{PMT}{(1+r)^2} + \frac{PMT}{(1+r)^3} + \cdots + \frac{PMT}{(1+r)^7} + \frac{PMT + FV}{(1+r)^8}$$

where:

PV = present value, or the price of the bond
PMT = coupon payment per period
FV = call price paid at call date
r = market discount rate, or required rate of return per period

$$101 = \frac{3}{(1+r)^1} + \frac{3}{(1+r)^2} + \frac{3}{(1+r)^3} + \cdots \frac{3}{(1+r)^7} + \frac{3+101}{(1+r)^8}$$

$r = 0.0297$

To arrive at the annualized yield-to-second-call, the semiannual rate of 2.97% must be multiplied by two. Therefore, the yield-to-second-call is equal to 2.97% × 2 = 5.94%.

30. B is correct. The yield-to-worst is 5.77%. The bond's yield-to-worst is the lowest of the sequence of yields-to-call and the yield-to-maturity. From above, we have the following yield measures for this bond:
Yield-to-first-call: 6.25%
Yield-to-second-call: 5.94%
Yield-to-maturity: 5.77%
Thus, the yield-to-worst is 5.77%.

31. B is correct. The discount or required margin is 236 bps. Given the floater has a maturity of two years and is linked to 6-month Libor, the formula for calculating discount margin is:

$$PV = \frac{\frac{(\text{Index} + QM) \times FV}{m}}{\left(1 + \frac{\text{Index} + DM}{m}\right)^1} + \frac{\frac{(\text{Index} + QM) \times FV}{m}}{\left(1 + \frac{\text{Index} + DM}{m}\right)^2} + \cdots + \frac{\frac{(\text{Index} + QM) \times FV}{m} + FV}{\left(1 + \frac{\text{Index} + DM}{m}\right)^4}$$

where:

PV = present value, or the price of the floating-rate note = 97
Index = reference rate, stated as an annual percentage rate = 0.01
QM = quoted margin, stated as an annual percentage rate = 0.0080
FV = future value paid at maturity, or the par value of the bond = 100
m = periodicity of the floating-rate note, the number of payment periods per year = 2
DM = discount margin, the required margin stated as an annual percentage rate

Substituting given values in:

$$97 = \frac{\frac{(0.01 + 0.0080) \times 100}{2}}{\left(1 + \frac{0.01 + DM}{2}\right)^1} + \frac{\frac{(0.01 + 0.0080) \times 100}{2}}{\left(1 + \frac{0.01 + DM}{2}\right)^2} + \cdots + \frac{\frac{(0.01 + 0.0080) \times 100}{2} + 100}{\left(1 + \frac{0.01 + DM}{2}\right)^4}$$

$$97 = \frac{0.90}{\left(1 + \frac{0.01 + DM}{2}\right)^1} + \frac{0.90}{\left(1 + \frac{0.01 + DM}{2}\right)^2} + \frac{0.90}{\left(1 + \frac{0.01 + DM}{2}\right)^3} + \frac{0.90 + 100}{\left(1 + \frac{0.01 + DM}{2}\right)^4}$$

To calculate DM, begin by solving for the discount rate per period:

$$97 = \frac{0.90}{(1+r)^1} + \frac{0.90}{(1+r)^2} + \frac{0.90}{(1+r)^3} + \frac{0.90 + 100}{(1+r)^4}$$

$$r = 0.0168$$

Now, solve for DM:

$$\frac{0.01 + DM}{2} = 0.0168$$

$$DM = 0.0236$$

The discount margin for the floater is equal to 236 bps.

32. A is correct. FRN X will be priced at a premium on the next reset date because the quoted margin of 0.40% is greater than the discount or required margin of 0.32%. The premium amount is the present value of the extra or "excess" interest payments of 0.08% each quarter (0.40% – 0.32%). FRN Y will be priced at par value on the next reset date since there is no difference between the quoted and discount margins. FRN Z will be priced at a discount since the quoted margin is less than the required margin.
33. C is correct. The bond equivalent yield is closest to 3.78%. It is calculated as:

$$AOR = \left(\frac{\text{Year}}{\text{Days}}\right) \times \left(\frac{FV - PV}{PV}\right)$$

where:

PV = present value, principal amount, or the price of the money market instrument
FV = future value, or the redemption amount paid at maturity including interest
Days = number of days between settlement and maturity
Year = number of days in the year
AOR = add-on rate, stated as an annual percentage rate (also, called bond equivalent yield)

$$AOR = \left(\frac{365}{350}\right) \times \left(\frac{100 - 96.5}{96.5}\right)$$

$$AOR = 1.04286 \times 0.03627$$

$$AOR = 0.03783 \text{ or approximately } 3.78\%$$

34. C is correct. The bond equivalent yield is closest to 4.40%. The present value of the banker's acceptance is calculated as:

$$PV = FV \times \left(1 - \frac{\text{Days}}{\text{Year}} \times DR\right)$$

where:

PV = present value, or price of the money market instrument
FV = future value paid at maturity, or face value of the money market instrument
Days = number of days between settlement and maturity
Year = number of days in the year
DR = discount rate, stated as an annual percentage rate

$$PV = 100 \times \left(1 - \frac{\text{Days}}{\text{Year}} \times DR\right)$$

$$PV = 100 \times \left(1 - \frac{180}{360} \times 0.0425\right)$$

$$PV = 100 \times (1 - 0.02125)$$

$$PV = 100 \times 0.97875$$

$$PV = 97.875$$

The bond equivalent yield (AOR) is calculated as:

$$AOR = \left(\frac{\text{Year}}{\text{Days}}\right) \times \left(\frac{FV - PV}{PV}\right)$$

where:

PV = present value, principal amount, or the price of the money market instrument
FV = future value, or the redemption amount paid at maturity including interest
Days = number of days between settlement and maturity
Year = number of days in the year
AOR = add-on rate (bond equivalent yield), stated as an annual percentage rate

$$AOR = \left(\frac{365}{180}\right) \times \left(\frac{100 - PV}{PV}\right)$$

$$AOR = \left(\frac{365}{180}\right) \times \left(\frac{100 - 97.875}{97.875}\right)$$

$$AOR = 2.02778 \times 0.02171$$

$$AOR = 0.04402, \text{ or approximately } 4.40\%$$

Note that the PV is calculated using an assumed 360-day year and the AOR (bond equivalent yield) is calculated using a 365-day year.

35. B is correct. All bonds on a par curve are assumed to have similar, not different, credit risk. Par curves are obtained from spot curves, and all bonds used to derive the par curve are assumed to have the same credit risk, as well as the same periodicity, currency, liquidity, tax status, and annual yields. A par curve is a sequence of yields-to-maturity such that each bond is priced at par value.
36. B is correct. The spot curve, also known as the strip or zero curve, is the yield curve constructed from a sequence of yields-to-maturities on zero-coupon bonds. The par curve is a sequence of yields-to-maturity such that each bond is priced at par value. The forward curve is constructed using a series of forward rates, each having the same time frame.
37. B is correct. The forward rate can be interpreted to be the incremental or marginal return for extending the time-to-maturity of an investment for an additional time period. The add-on rate (bond equivalent yield) is a rate quoted for money market instruments such as bank certificates of deposit and indices such as Libor and Euribor. Yield-to-maturity is the internal rate of return on the bond's cash flows—the uniform interest rate such that when the bond's future cash flows are discounted at that rate, the sum of the present values equals the price of the bond. It is the implied market discount rate.
38. B is correct. The 3 year implied spot rate is closest to 1.94%. It is calculated as the geometric average of the one-year forward rates:

$$(1.0080 \times 1.0112 \times 1.0394) = (1 + z_3)^3$$
$$1.05945 = (1 + z_3)^3$$
$$[1.05945]^{1/3} = [(1 + z_3)^3]^{1/3}$$
$$1.01944 = 1 + z_3$$
$$1.01944 - 1 = z_3$$
$$0.01944 = z_3,\ z_3 = 1.944\% \text{ or approximately } 1.94\%$$

39. B is correct. The value per 100 of par value is closest to 105.01. Using the forward curve, the bond price is calculated as follows:

$$\frac{3.5}{1.0080} + \frac{103.5}{(1.0080 \times 1.0112)} = 3.47 + 101.54 = 105.01$$

40. C is correct. The spread component of a specific bond's yield-to-maturity is least likely impacted by changes in inflation of its currency of denomination. The effect of changes in macroeconomic factors, such as the expected rate of inflation in the currency of denomination, is seen mostly in changes in the benchmark yield. The spread or risk premium component is impacted by microeconomic factors specific to the bond and bond issuer including tax status and quality rating.
41. A is correct. The I-spread, or interpolated spread, is the yield spread of a specific bond over the standard swap rate in that currency of the same tenor. The yield spread in basis points over an actual or interpolated government bond is known as the G-spread. The Z-spread (zero-volatility spread) is the constant spread such that is added to each spot rate such that the present value of the cash flows matches the price of the bond.
42. B is correct. The G-spread is closest to 285 bps. The benchmark rate for UK fixed-rate bonds is the UK government benchmark bond. The euro interest rate spread benchmark

is used to calculate the G-spread for euro-denominated corporate bonds, not UK bonds. The G-spread is calculated as follows:

Yield-to-maturity on the UK corporate bond:

$$100.65 = \frac{5}{(1+r)^1} + \frac{5}{(1+r)^2} + \frac{105}{(1+r)^3},\ r = 0.04762 \text{ or } 476 \text{ bps}$$

Yield-to-maturity on the UK government benchmark bond:

$$100.25 = \frac{2}{(1+r)^1} + \frac{2}{(1+r)^2} + \frac{102}{(1+r)^3},\ r = 0.01913 \text{ or } 191 \text{ bps}$$

The G-spread is 476 – 191 = 285 bps.

43. A is correct. The value of the bond is closest to 92.38. The calculation is:

$$PV = \frac{PMT}{(1+z_1+Z)^1} + \frac{PMT}{(1+z_2+Z)^2} + \frac{PMT+FV}{(1+z_3+Z)^3}$$

$$= \frac{5}{(1+0.0486+0.0234)^1} + \frac{5}{(1+0.0495+0.0234)^2} + \frac{105}{(1+0.0565+0.0234)^3}$$

$$= \frac{5}{1.0720} + \frac{5}{1.15111} + \frac{105}{1.25936} = 4.66 + 4.34 + 83.38 = 92.38$$

44. C is correct. The option value in basis points per year is subtracted from the Z-spread to calculate the option-adjusted spread (OAS). The Z-spread is the constant yield spread over the benchmark spot curve. The I-spread is the yield spread of a specific bond over the standard swap rate in that currency of the same tenor.

CHAPTER 4

UNDERSTANDING FIXED-INCOME RISK AND RETURN

SOLUTIONS

1. A is correct. A capital gain is least likely to contribute to the investor's total return. There is no capital gain (or loss) because the bond is held to maturity. The carrying value of the bond at maturity is par value, the same as the redemption amount. When a fixed-rate bond is held to its maturity, the investor receives the principal payment at maturity. This principal payment is a source of return for the investor. A fixed-rate bond pays periodic coupon payments, and the reinvestment of these coupon payments is a source of return for the investor. The investor's total return is the redemption of principal at maturity and the sum of the reinvested coupons.
2. C is correct. Because the fixed-rate bond is held to maturity (a "buy-and-hold" investor), interest rate risk arises entirely from changes in coupon reinvestment rates. Higher interest rates increase income from reinvestment of coupon payments, and lower rates decrease income from coupon reinvestment. There will not be a capital gain or loss because the bond is held until maturity. The carrying value at the maturity date is par value, the same as the redemption amount. The redemption of principal does not expose the investor to interest rate risk. The risk to a bond's principal is credit risk.
3. A is correct. Capital gains (losses) arise if a bond is sold at a price above (below) its constant-yield price trajectory. A point on the trajectory represents the carrying value of the bond at that time. That is, the capital gain/loss is measured from the bond's carrying value, the point on the constant-yield price trajectory, and not from the original purchase price. The carrying value is the original purchase price plus the amortized amount of the discount if the bond is purchased at a price below par value. If the bond is purchased at a price above par value, the carrying value is the original purchase price minus (not plus) the amortized amount of the premium. The amortized amount for each year is the change in the price between two points on the trajectory.

4. C is correct. The future value of reinvested cash flows at 8% after five years is closest to 41.07 per 100 of par value.

$$\left[7\times(1.08)^4\right]+\left[7\times(1.08)^3\right]+\left[7\times(1.08)^2\right]+\left[7\times(1.08)^1\right]+7=41.0662$$

The 6.07 difference between the sum of the coupon payments over the five-year holding period (35) and the future value of the reinvested coupons (41.07) represents the "interest-on-interest" gain from compounding.

5. B is correct. The capital loss is closest to 3.31 per 100 of par value. After five years, the bond has four years remaining until maturity and the sale price of the bond is 96.69, calculated as:

$$\frac{7}{(1.08)^1}+\frac{7}{(1.08)^2}+\frac{7}{(1.08)^3}+\frac{107}{(1.08)^4}=96.69$$

The investor purchased the bond at a price equal to par value (100). Because the bond was purchased at a price equal to its par value, the carrying value is par value. Therefore, the investor experienced a capital loss of 96.69 – 100 = –3.31.

6. B is correct. The investor's five-year horizon yield is closest to 6.62%. After five years, the sale price of the bond is 96.69 (from problem 5) and the future value of reinvested cash flows at 6% is 41.0662 (from problem 4) per 100 of par value. The total return is 137.76 (= 41.07 + 96.69), resulting in a realized five-year horizon yield of 6.62%:

$$100.00=\frac{137.76}{(1+r)^5}, \qquad r=0.0662$$

7. A is correct. The bond's approximate modified duration is closest to 2.78. Approximate modified duration is calculated as:

$$\text{ApproxModDur}=\frac{(PV_-)-(PV_+)}{2\times(\Delta\text{Yield})\times(PV_0)}$$

Lower yield-to-maturity by 5 bps to 2.95%:

$$PV_-=\frac{5}{(1+0.0295)^1}+\frac{5}{(1+0.0295)^2}+\frac{5+100}{(1+0.0295)^3}=105.804232$$

Increase yield-to-maturity by 5 bps to 3.05%:

$$PV_+=\frac{5}{(1+0.0305)^1}+\frac{5}{(1+0.0305)^2}+\frac{5+100}{(1+0.0305)^3}=105.510494$$

$PV_0 = 105.657223$, $\Delta\text{Yield} = 0.0005$

$$\text{ApproxModDur}=\frac{105.804232-105.510494}{2\times0.0005\times105.657223}=2.78$$

8. C is correct. A bond's modified duration cannot be larger than its Macaulay duration. The formula for modified duration is:

$$\text{ModDur}=\frac{\text{MacDur}}{1+r}$$

where r is the bond's yield-to-maturity per period. A bond's yield-to-maturity has an effective lower bound of 0, and thus the denominator $1 + r$ term has a lower bound of 1. Therefore, ModDur will typically be less than MacDur.

Effective duration is a measure of curve duration. Modified duration is a measure of yield duration.

9. C is correct. The bond's Macaulay duration is closest to 2.83. Macaulay duration (MacDur) is a weighted average of the times to the receipt of cash flow. The weights are the shares of the full price corresponding to each coupon and principal payment.

Period	Cash Flow	Present Value	Weight	Period × Weight
1	6	5.555556	0.058575	0.058575
2	6	5.144033	0.054236	0.108472
3	106	84.146218	0.887190	2.661570
		94.845806	1.000000	2.828617

Thus, the bond's Macaulay duration (MacDur) is 2.83.

Alternatively, Macaulay duration can be calculated using the following closed-form formula:

$$\text{MacDur} = \left\{\frac{1+r}{r} - \frac{1+r+\left[N\times(c-r)\right]}{c\times\left[(1+r)^N-1\right]+r}\right\} - (t/T)$$

$$\text{MacDur} = \left\{\frac{1.08}{0.08} - \frac{1.08+\left[3\times(0.06-0.08)\right]}{0.06\times\left[(1.08)^3-1\right]+0.08}\right\} - 0$$

$$\text{MacDur} = 13.50 - 10.67 = 2.83$$

10. A is correct. The interest rate risk of a fixed-rate bond with an embedded call option is best measured by effective duration. A callable bond's future cash flows are uncertain because they are contingent on future interest rates. The issuer's decision to call the bond depends on future interest rates. Therefore, the yield-to-maturity on a callable bond is not well defined. Only effective duration, which takes into consideration the value of the call option, is the appropriate interest rate risk measure. Yield durations like Macaulay and modified durations are not relevant for a callable bond because they assume no changes in cash flows when interest rates change.

11. A is correct. Key rate duration is used to measure a bond's sensitivity to a shift at one or more maturity segments of the yield curve which result in a change to yield curve shape. Modified and effective duration measure a bond's sensitivity to parallel shifts in the entire curve.

12. B is correct. The effective duration of the pension fund's liabilities is closest to 14.99. The effective duration is calculated as follows:

$$\text{EffDur} = \frac{(PV_-)-(PV_+)}{2\times(\Delta\text{Curve})\times(PV_0)}$$

$PV_0 = 455.4$, $PV_+ = 373.6$, $PV_- = 510.1$, and $\Delta\text{Curve} = 0.0100$.

$$\text{EffDur} = \frac{510.1-373.6}{2\times0.0100\times455.4} = 14.99$$

13. B is correct. A bond's yield-to-maturity is inversely related to its Macaulay duration: The higher the yield-to-maturity, the lower its Macaulay duration and the lower the interest rate risk. A higher yield-to-maturity decreases the weighted average of the times to the receipt of cash flow, and thus decreases the Macaulay duration.

    A bond's coupon rate is inversely related to its Macaulay duration: The lower the coupon, the greater the weight of the payment of principal at maturity. This results in a higher Macaulay duration. Zero-coupon bonds do not pay periodic coupon payments; therefore, the Macaulay duration of a zero-coupon bond is its time-to-maturity.
14. A is correct. The presence of an embedded put option reduces the effective duration of the bond, especially when rates are rising. If interest rates are low compared with the coupon rate, the value of the put option is low and the impact of the change in the benchmark yield on the bond's price is very similar to the impact on the price of a non-putable bond. But when benchmark interest rates rise, the put option becomes more valuable to the investor. The ability to sell the bond at par value limits the price depreciation as rates rise. The presence of an embedded put option reduces the sensitivity of the bond price to changes in the benchmark yield, assuming no change in credit risk.
15. A is correct. The portfolio's modified duration is closest to 7.62. Portfolio duration is commonly estimated as the market-value-weighted average of the yield durations of the individual bonds that compose the portfolio.

    The total market value of the bond portfolio is 170,000 + 120,000 + 100,000 = 390,000.

    The portfolio duration is 5.42 × (170,000/390,000) + 8.44 × (120,000/390,000) + 10.38 × (100,000/390,000) = 7.62.
16. A is correct. A limitation of calculating a bond portfolio's duration as the weighted average of the yield durations of the individual bonds is that this measure implicitly assumes a parallel shift to the yield curve (all rates change by the same amount in the same direction). In reality, interest rate changes frequently result in a steeper or flatter yield curve. This approximation of the "theoretically correct" portfolio duration is *more* accurate when the yield curve is flatter (less steeply sloped). An advantage of this approach is that it can be used with portfolios that include bonds with embedded options. Bonds with embedded options can be included in the weighted average using the effective durations for these securities.
17. B is correct. Bond B has the greatest money duration per 100 of par value. Money duration (MoneyDur) is calculated as the annual modified duration *(AnnModDur)* times the full price (PV^{Full}) of the bond including accrued interest. Bond B has the highest money duration per 100 of par value.

$$\text{MoneyDur} = \text{AnnModDur} \times PV^{Full}$$

$$\text{MoneyDur of Bond A} = 5.42 \times 85.00 = 460.70$$

$$\text{MoneyDur of Bond B} = 8.44 \times 80.00 = 675.20$$

$$\text{MoneyDur of Bond C} = 7.54 \times 85.78 = 646.78$$

18. B is correct. The PVBP is closest to 0.0648. The formula for the price value of a basis point is:

$$\text{PVBP} = \frac{(PV_-) - (PV_+)}{2}$$

where:

PVBP = price value of a basis point
PV_- = full price calculated by lowering the yield-to-maturity by one basis point
PV_+ = full price calculated by raising the yield-to-maturity by one basis point

Lowering the yield-to-maturity by one basis point to 4.99% results in a bond price of 85.849134:

$$PV_- = \frac{3}{(1+0.0499)^1} + \cdots + \frac{3+100}{(1+0.0499)^9} = 85.849134$$

Increasing the yield-to-maturity by one basis point to 5.01% results in a bond price of 85.719638:

$$PV_+ = \frac{3}{(1+0.0501)^1} + \cdots + \frac{3+100}{(1+0.0501)^9} = 85.719638$$

$$\text{PVBP} = \frac{85.849134 - 85.719638}{2} = 0.06475$$

Alternatively, the PVBP can be derived using modified duration:

$$\text{ApproxModDur} = \frac{(PV_-) - (PV_+)}{2 \times (\Delta\text{Yield}) \times (PV_0)}$$

$$\text{ApproxModDur} = \frac{85.849134 - 85.719638}{2 \times 0.0001 \times 85.784357} = 7.548$$

$$\text{PVBP} = 7.548 \times 85.784357 \times 0.0001 = 0.06475$$

19. B is correct. Convexity measures the "second order" effect on a bond's percentage price change given a change in yield-to-maturity. Convexity adjusts the percentage price change estimate provided by modified duration to better approximate the true relationship between a bond's price and its yield-to-maturity which is a curved line (convex).

    Duration estimates the change in the bond's price along the straight line that is tangent to this curved line ("first order" effect). Yield volatility measures the magnitude of changes in the yields along the yield curve.
20. B is correct. The bond's approximate convexity is closest to 70.906. Approximate convexity (ApproxCon) is calculated using the following formula:

$$\text{ApproxCon} = [PV_- + PV_+ - (2 \times PV_0)]/(\Delta\text{Yield}^2 \times PV_0)$$

where:

PV_- = new price when the yield-to-maturity is decreased
PV_+ = new price when the yield-to-maturity is increased
PV_0 = original price
ΔYield = change in yield-to-maturity

$$\text{ApproxCon} = [98.782 + 98.669 - (2 \times 98.722)]/(0.001^2 \times 98.722) = 70.906$$

21. C is correct. The expected percentage price change is closest to 1.78%. The convexity-adjusted percentage price change for a bond given a change in the yield-to-maturity is estimated by:

$$\%\Delta PV^{Full} \approx [-\text{AnnModDur} \times \Delta\text{Yield}] + [0.5 \times \text{AnnConvexity} \times (\Delta\text{Yield})^2]$$

$$\%\Delta PV^{Full} \approx [-7.020 \times (-0.0025)] + [0.5 \times 65.180 \times (-0.0025)^2] = 0.017754, \text{ or } 1.78\%$$

22. B is correct. The expected percentage price change is closest to –3.49%. The convexity-adjusted percentage price change for a bond given a change in the yield-to-maturity is estimated by:

$$\%\Delta PV^{Full} \approx [-\text{AnnModDur} \times \Delta\text{Yield}] + [0.5 \times \text{AnnConvexity} \times (\Delta\text{Yield})^2]$$

$$\%\Delta PV^{Full} \approx [-7.140 \times 0.005] + [0.5 \times 66.200 \times (0.005)^2] = -0.034873, \text{ or } -3.49\%$$

23. B is correct. If the term structure of yield volatility is downward-sloping, then short-term bond yields-to-maturity have greater volatility than for long-term bonds. Therefore, long-term yields are more stable than short-term yields. Higher volatility in short-term rates does not necessarily mean that the level of short-term rates is higher than long-term rates. With a downward-sloping term structure of yield volatility, short-term bonds will not always experience greater price fluctuation than long-term bonds. The estimated percentage change in a bond price depends on the modified duration and convexity as well as on the yield-to-maturity change.
24. C is correct. When the holder of a bond experiences a one-time parallel shift in the yield curve, the Macaulay duration statistic identifies the number of years necessary to hold the bond so that the losses (or gains) from coupon reinvestment offset the gains (or losses) from market price changes. The duration gap is the difference between the Macaulay duration and the investment horizon. Modified duration approximates the percentage price change of a bond given a change in its yield-to-maturity.
25. C is correct. The duration gap is equal to the bond's Macaulay duration minus the investment horizon. In this case, the duration gap is positive, and price risk dominates coupon reinvestment risk. The investor risk is to higher rates.

    The investor is hedged against interest rate risk if the duration gap is zero; that is, the investor's investment horizon is equal to the bond's Macaulay duration. The investor is at risk of lower rates only if the duration gap is negative; that is, the investor's investment horizon is greater than the bond's Macaulay duration. In this case, coupon reinvestment risk dominates market price risk.
26. C is correct. The duration gap is closest to 4.158. The duration gap is a bond's Macaulay duration minus the investment horizon. The approximate Macaulay duration is the approximate modified duration times one plus the yield-to-maturity. It is 12.158 (= 11.470 × 1.06).

    Given an investment horizon of eight years, the duration gap for this bond at purchase is positive: 12.158 – 8 = 4.158. When the investment horizon is less than the Macaulay duration of the bond, the duration gap is positive, and price risk dominates coupon reinvestment risk.
27. A is correct. The price increase was most likely caused by a decrease in the bond's credit spread. The ratings upgrade most likely reflects a lower expected probability of default and/or a greater level of recovery of assets if default occurs. The decrease in credit risk results in a smaller credit spread. The increase in the bond price reflects a decrease in the yield-to-maturity due to a smaller credit spread. The change in the bond price was not due to a change in liquidity risk or an increase in the benchmark rate.

CHAPTER 5

FUNDAMENTALS OF CREDIT ANALYSIS

SOLUTIONS

1. A is correct. Credit migration risk or downgrade risk refers to the risk that a bond issuer's creditworthiness may deteriorate or migrate lower. The result is that investors view the risk of default to be higher, causing the spread on the issuer's bonds to widen.
2. C is correct. Market liquidity risk refers to the risk that the price at which investors transact may be different from the price indicated in the market. Market liquidity risk is increased by (1) less debt outstanding and/or (2) a lower issue credit rating. Because Stedsmart Ltd is comparable to Fignermo Ltd except for less publicly traded debt outstanding, it should have higher market liquidity risk.
3. B is correct. Unsecured bonds are often referred to as debentures. Unsecured debt holders only have a general claim on the issuer's assets and cash flow and have a lower priority claim than secured debt holders. Secured debt holders have a direct claim on certain assets and their associated cash flows.
4. A is correct. First mortgage debt is senior secured debt and has the highest priority of claims. First mortgage debt also has the highest expected recovery rate. First mortgage debt refers to the pledge of specific property. Neither senior unsecured nor junior subordinate debt has any claims on specific assets.
5. B is correct. Whether or not secured assets are sufficient for the claims against them does not influence priority of claims. Any deficiency between pledged assets and the claims against them becomes senior unsecured debt and still adheres to the guidelines of priority of claims.
6. C is correct. Both analysts and ratings agencies have difficulty foreseeing future debt-financed acquisitions.
7. C is correct. Goodwill is viewed as a lower quality asset compared with tangible assets that can be sold and more easily converted into cash.
8. C is correct. The value of assets in relation to the level of debt is important to assess the collateral of the company; that is, the quality and value of the assets that support the debt levels of the company.

9. B is correct. The growth prospects of the industry provide the analyst insight regarding the capacity of the company.
10. A is correct. The construction company is both highly leveraged, which increases credit risk, and in a highly cyclical industry, which results in more volatile earnings.
11. B is correct. The interest expense is €113 million and EBITDA = Operating profit + Depreciation and amortization = €894 + 249 million = €1,143 million. EBITDA interest coverage = EBITDA/Interest expense = 1,143/113 = 10.12 times.
12. B is correct. Total debt is €1,613 million with Total capital = Total debt + Shareholders' equity = €1,613 + 4,616 = €6,229 million. The Debt/Capital ratio = 1,613/6,229 = 25.90%.
13. A is correct. If the debt of the company remained unchanged but FFO increased, more cash is available to service debt compared to the previous year. Additionally, the debt/capital ratio has improved. It would imply that the ability of Pay Handle Ltd to service their debt has improved.
14. A is correct. Based on four of the five credit ratios, Grupa Zywiec SA's credit quality is superior to that of the industry.
15. A is correct. Davide Campari-Milano S.p.A. has more financial leverage and less interest coverage than Associated British Foods plc, which implies greater credit risk.
16. A is correct. Low demand implies wider yield spreads, while heavy supply will widen spreads even further.

CHAPTER 6

CREDIT ANALYSIS MODELS

SOLUTIONS

1. B is correct. Limitation B is incorrect. Credit ratings tend to be stable, not variable, across time and across the business cycle. Rating agencies may be motivated to keep their ratings stable across time to reduce unnecessary volatility in debt market prices. Credit ratings do not explicitly depend on the business cycle.

   The issuer-pays model for compensating credit rating agencies has a potential conflict of interest that may distort the accuracy of credit ratings. Credit ratings do not provide an estimate of default probability. They are ordinal rankings. There is no constant relationship between credit ratings and default probabilities.
2. B is correct. Holding the company's equity is economically equivalent to owning a European call option on the firm's assets. Holding the company's equity has the same payoff as a European call option on the company's assets with a strike price equivalent to the face value of the company's debt.
3. C is correct. The reduced form model assumes that some of the company's debt is traded. Reduced form models do not assume that the company's assets, equity, or all its debt are traded. The structural model assumes that the company's assets trade.
4. B is correct. The ability to use historical estimation is a significant advantage of the reduced form model. Both structural and reduced form models can use implicit estimation (or calibration).
5. A is correct. The reduced form model produces credit risk measures that reflect the changing business cycle. The credit risk measures from structural models do not explicitly depend on the business cycle. Credit ratings are also generally insensitive to changes in the business cycle. The reduced form model requires a specification of the company's balance sheet. Both reduced form and structural models can be used to estimate the expected present value of expected loss.
6. C is correct. The present value of the expected loss due to credit risk is closest to 18.00. It is the difference between the credit-adjusted valuation (present value) of 998.1623 and the risk-free valuation (risk-free present value) of 1,016.1606. [1,016.1606 - 998.1623 = 17.9983 ≈ 18.00]

7. A is correct. The present value of the expected loss due to credit risk is 0.04 and is calculated as the risk-free present value of 4.3450 less the risk-adjusted present value of 4.3042, or 0.0408, or approximately 0.04. [$4.3450 - 4.3042 = 0.0408 \approx 0.04$]
8. A is correct. Statement 1 is incorrect. The probability of default does not apply to ABS because asset-backed securities do not default when an interest payment is not made. Probability of loss is used in place of default. Credit analysis for both ABS and corporate bonds is different due to their future cash flow structures. Both structural and reduced form models can be used to analyze ABS and corporate bonds.

CHAPTER 7

INTRODUCTION TO ASSET-BACKED SECURITIES

SOLUTIONS

1. B is correct. Securitization increases the funds available for banks to lend because they no longer have to hold all the loans they originate on their balance sheet. The securitization process allows banks to remove loans from their balance sheets and issue bonds that are backed by those loans with the participation of several new entities. Securitization repackages relatively simple debt obligations, such as bank loans, into more complex structures. The process of securitization involves moving or selling assets from the owner of the assets—in this case, the banks—into a special legal entity called a special purpose vehicle (SPV).

   A is incorrect because securitization is a process in which simple debt obligations, such as bank loans, are repackaged into more complex (not simpler) structures.

   C is incorrect because the process of securitization involves moving or selling assets from the owner of the assets, in this case, the banks, into a special legal entity. A special purpose vehicle (SPV) is the legal entity that issues and sells the asset-backed bonds.
2. A is correct. In a securitization, a special purpose vehicle (SPV) is the special legal entity responsible for the issuance of the asset-backed securities. In a prospectus for a securitization, the SPV is referred to as either the "issuer" or the "trust." The originator or depositor sells assets (loans or receivables) to the SPV for cash. The SPV obtains the cash used to pay the originator by selling asset-backed securities that are backed or collateralized by the originator's assets. The servicer is responsible for both the collection of payments from the borrowers and the recovery of underlying assets for delinquent loans.

   B is incorrect because the servicer (not the SPV) is responsible for the collection of payments from the borrowers.

   C is incorrect because the servicer (not the SPV) is responsible for recovery of the underlying assets from borrowers who are delinquent.
3. A is correct. Time tranching is the process in which a set of bond classes or tranches is created that allow investors a choice in the type of prepayment risk, extension or contraction, that they prefer to bear. Senior and subordinate bond classes are used in credit tranching

structures as a form of credit enhancement. Credit tranching structures allow investors to choose the amount of credit risk that they prefer to bear.

B is incorrect because fully and partially amortizing loans are the two types of amortizing loans. Amortization is a loan specification or design and refers to how the principal on a loan is repaid.

C is incorrect because senior and subordinate bond classes are used in credit tranching structures as a means of credit enhancement. Credit tranching structures redistribute the credit risk associated with the underlying collateral and allow investors to choose the amount of credit risk that they prefer to bear.

4. B is correct. Bank Nederlandse has a claim against Marolf for 1.5 million EUR, the shortfall between the amount of the mortgage balance outstanding and the proceeds received from the sale of the property. This indicates that the mortgage loan is a recourse loan. The recourse/non-recourse feature indicates the rights of a lender in foreclosure. If Marolf had a non-recourse loan, the bank would have only been entitled to the proceeds from the sale of the underlying property, or 2.5 million EUR.

   A is incorrect because a bullet loan is a special type of interest-only mortgage for which there are no scheduled principal payments over the entire term of the loan. Since the unpaid balance is less than the original mortgage loan, it is unlikely that Marolf has an interest-only mortgage.

   C is incorrect because Bank Nederlandse has a claim against Marolf for the shortfall between the amount of the mortgage balance outstanding and the proceeds received from the sale of the property. A non-recourse loan limits the rights of a lender in a foreclosure to the proceeds from the sale of the underlying property.

5. A is correct. Because the loan has a non-recourse feature, the lender can only look to the underlying property to recover the outstanding mortgage balance and has no further claim against the borrower. The lender is simply entitled to foreclose on the home and sell it.

   B and C are incorrect because the lender would be entitled to claim the shortfall between the mortgage balance outstanding and the proceeds received from the sale of the property only if the loan was of the recourse (not non-recourse) type.

6. B is correct. The difference between the $10,000 monthly mortgage payment and the $2,500 portion of the payment that represents interest equals $7,500, which is the amount of the total required payment applied to reduce the outstanding mortgage balance. In addition, a payment made in excess of the monthly mortgage payment is called a prepayment. The prepayment of $5,000 is a partial pay down of the mortgage balance. The outstanding mortgage balance after the $15,000 payment is the 01/01/2014 mortgage balance of $500,000 – $7,500 – $5,000 = $487,500.

   A is incorrect because $485,000 is calculated by subtracting the total mortgage payment of $10,000 plus the prepayment of $5,000 from the outstanding mortgage balance of $500,000. The outstanding mortgage balance should not be reduced by the $2,500 interest component.

   C is incorrect because $490,000 is calculated by subtracting only the total required mortgage payment of $10,000 from the outstanding mortgage balance of $500,000, which ignores the interest component of the total required payment.

7. A is correct. Non-agency RMBS are credit enhanced, either internally or externally. The most common forms of internal credit enhancements are senior/subordinate structures, reserve funds, and overcollateralization. Conforming mortgages are used as collateral for agency (not non-agency) mortgage pass-through securities. An agency RMBS, rather than

a non-agency RMBS, issued by a GSE (government sponsored enterprise), is guaranteed by the respective GSE.

B is incorrect because non-conforming (not comforming) mortgages are used as collateral for non-agency mortgage pass-through securities. To be included in a pool of loans backing an agency RMBS, it must meet specified underwriting standards. If a loan satisfies the underwriting standards for inclusion as collateral for an agency mortgage-backed security, it is called a conforming mortgage. If a loan fails to satisfy the underwriting standards, it is called a non-conforming loan.

C is incorrect because an agency RMBS, rather than a non-agency RMBS, issued by a GSE (government sponsored enterprise), is guaranteed by the respective GSE. The RMBS issued by GSEs are those issued by Fannie Mae (previously referred to as the Federal National Mortgage Association) and Freddie Mac (previously referred to as the Federal Home Loan Mortgage Corporation).

8. B is correct. The cash flow of the underlying mortgage pool consists of monthly mortgage payments representing interest, the scheduled repayment of principal, and any prepayments. The monthly cash flow for a pass-through security is less than the monthly cash flow of the underlying pool by an amount equal to servicing and other fees. The other fees are those charged by the issuer or guarantor of the pass-through for guaranteeing the issue. The gross interest is calculated using the weighted average coupon (WAC) rate for the mortgage loans in the pool. The total cash flow to be received by the investors is $1,910,542 of total principal plus the $3,562,500 gross coupon interest less servicing and other fees, or $1,910,542 + $3,562,500 – $337,500 – $58,333 = $5,077,029.

   A is incorrect because the $4,473,042 is calculated by adding the scheduled principal payments of $910,542 to the gross coupon interest of $3,562,500. The cash flow for a pass-through security is the mortgage cash flow of the underlying mortgage pool, which includes the scheduled repayment of principal, any prepayments, and gross coupon interest less the amount equal to servicing and other fees.

   C is incorrect because $5,473,042 is calculated by adding the total principal of $1,910,542 to the gross interest of $3,562,500. The monthly cash flow for a pass-through is less than the monthly cash flow of the underlying pool by an amount equal to servicing and other fees which total $337,500 + $58,333 = 395,833.

9. B is correct. CPR is an annualized rate that indicates the percentage of the mortgage balance at the beginning of the year, which is expected to be prepaid by the end of the year. The single monthly mortality rate (SMM) is a monthly measure of the percentage of the mortgage balance available to prepay for a pool of mortgages that is projected to prepay in the given month. The prepayment rate over the life of mortgages in the mortgage pool could only be computed at the end of the life of the mortgages.

   A is incorrect because the single monthly mortality rate (SMM), not the CPR, is the percentage of the outstanding mortgage balance available to prepay for a pool of mortgages at the beginning of the month that is projected to prepay that month.

   C is incorrect because the prepayment rate over the life of the mortgages in a mortgage pool could only be computed at the end of the life of the mortgages and therefore can only be projected based on an assumed prepayment rate.

10. C is correct. When interest rates decline, a pass-through security is subject to contraction risk. Contraction risk is the risk that the security will be shorter in maturity than was anticipated when the security was purchased due to higher than expected prepayments (which typically occurs when interest rates decline). Extension risk is the risk that when interest rates rise, there are fewer prepayments and, as a result, the security becomes longer

in maturity than anticipated at the time of purchase. Balloon risk (common with commercial mortgage-backed securities), a type of extension risk, is the risk that a borrower will not be able to make the balloon payment when due.

A is incorrect because balloon risk is a type of extension risk. A pass-through security is subject to extension risk when interest rates rise (not decline).

B is incorrect because extension risk is the risk that when interest rates rise (not decline), there are fewer prepayments and, as a result, the security becomes longer in maturity than anticipated at the time of purchase.

11. A is correct. From a lender's perspective, balloon risk refers to the risk that a borrower will not be able to make the balloon payment when due. Since the term of the loan will be extended by the lender during the workout period, balloon risk is a type of extension risk. Extension risk is the undesired lengthening in the expected life of a security.

    B is incorrect because balloon risk is a type of extension (not contraction) risk. Contraction risk would be the risk that the security will be shorter in maturity than was anticipated when the security was purchased.

    C is incorrect because, from the lender's perpective, balloon risk relates to the undesired lengthening in the expected life of the security (extension risk). A borrower (not the lender) may face interest rate risk if planning to refinance the balloon amount on the balloon payment date. The interest rate on a new loan to refinance the balloon balance on the balloon payment date is unknown, and thus the borrower is exposed to interest rate risk.

12. A is correct. Because commercial mortgage loans are non-recourse loans, the lender can only look to the income-producing property backing the loan for interest and principal repayment. If there is a default, the lender looks to the proceeds from the sale of the property for repayment and has no recourse against the borrower for any unpaid mortgage loan balance. Call protection addresses prepayment risk. Investors have considerable call protection at both the structure and the loan level with CMBS. At the loan level, there are four mechanisms that offer investors call protection: prepayment penalty points, prepayment lockouts, yield maintenance charges, and defeasance.

    B is incorrect because call protection addresses prepayment risk. Investors have considerable call protection at both the structure and the loan level with CMBS.

    C is incorrect because at the loan level there are four mechanisms that offer investors call protection: prepayment penalty points, prepayment lockouts, yield maintenance, and defeasance.

13. A is correct. With CMBS, investors have considerable call protection. An investor in a RMBS is exposed to considerable prepayment risk, but with CMBS, call protection is available to the investor at both the structure and the loan level. The call protection results in CMBS trading in the market more like a corporate bond than an RMBS. Both internal credit enhancement and the debt-to-service coverage (DSC) ratio address credit risk, not prepayment risk. Internal credit enhancements are available for CMBS, but are not needed for an agency RMBS, which is issued with a guarantee by its respective GSE. The DSC ratio level is used as a key indicator of the potential credit performance of the property underlying a commercial mortgage loan.

    B is incorrect because an internal credit enhancement mechanism such as "subordination" is used to achieve desired rating levels for a CMBS. An agency RMBS is guaranteed by the respective GSE and does not require a credit enhancement mechanism to reduce credit risk. Both credit enhancement and government guarantees address credit risk, not prepayment risk.

C is incorrect because the debt-to-service coverage (DSC) ratio level is used as a key indicator of the potential credit performance of the property underlying a commercial mortgage loan. If certain DSC levels are needed, then an internal credit enhancement mechanism is used to achieve a desired rating level. The loan-to-value ratio is used for residential mortgage loans. Both ratios are indicators of credit performance and do not address prepayment risk.

14. A is correct. Because of credit risk, all structures have some form of credit enhancement. An excess spread account is a form of internal credit enhancement that involves the allocation of any amounts into an account resulting from monthly funds remaining after paying out the interest to the bond classes, servicing fees, and administrative fees. The excess spread is a design feature of the structure. Time tranching (not an excess spread account) addresses prepayment risk (extension or contraction) to allow investors a choice in the type of prepayment risk that they prefer to bear.

    B and C are incorrect because an excess spread account is a form of internal credit enhancement. Time tranching addresses prepayment risk (extension or contraction) to allow investors a choice in the type of prepayment risk that they prefer to bear.

15. B is correct. During the lockout period, the cash flow that is paid out to security holders is based only on finance charges collected and fees. After the lockout period, the principal is no longer reinvested but paid to investors.

    A and C are incorrect because, during the lockout period, the cash flow paid out to credit card receivable-backed security holders is based only on collected finance charges and fees. After the lockout period, the principal is no longer reinvested but paid to investors.

CHAPTER 8

THE ARBITRAGE-FREE VALUATION FRAMEWORK

SOLUTIONS

1. A is correct. This is the same bond being sold at three different prices, so an arbitrage opportunity exists by buying the bond from the exchange where it is priced lowest and immediately selling it on the exchange that has the highest price. Accordingly, an investor would maximize profit from the arbitrage opportunity by buying the bond on the Frankfurt exchange (which has the lowest price of €103.7565) and selling it on the Eurex exchange (which has the highest price of €103.7956) to generate a risk-free profit of €0.0391 (as mentioned, ignoring transaction costs) per €100 par.

   B is incorrect because buying on NYSE Euronext and selling on Eurex would result in an €0.0141 profit per €100 par (€103.7956 – €103.7815 = €0.0141), which is not the maximum arbitrage profit available. A greater profit would be realized if the bond were purchased in Frankfurt and sold on Eurex.

   C is incorrect because buying on Frankfurt and selling on NYSE Euronext would result in an €0.0250 profit per €100 par (€103.7815 – €103.7565 = €0.0250). A greater profit would be realized if the bond were purchased in Frankfurt and sold on Eurex.
2. C is correct. The bond from Exhibit 1 is selling for its calculated value on the NYSE Euronext exchange. The arbitrage-free value of a bond is the present value of its cash flows discounted by the spot rate for zero coupon bonds maturing on the same date as each cash flow. The value of this bond, 103.7815, is calculated as follows:

	Year 1	Year 2	Year 3	Total PV
Yield to maturity	1.2500%	1.500%	1.700%	
Spot rate[1]	1.2500%	1.5019%	1.7049%	
Cash flow	3.00	3.00	103.00	
Present value of payment[2]	2.9630	2.9119	97.9066	103.7815

(continued)

	Eurex	NYSE Euronext	Frankfurt
Price	€103.7956	€103.7815	€103.7565
Mispricing (per 100 par value)	0.141	0	–0.025

Notes:

[1] Spot rates calculated using bootstrapping; for example: Year 2 spot rate (z_2): 100 = 1.5/1.0125 + $101.5/(1 + z_2)^2 = 0.015019$.

[2] Present value calculated using the formula $PV = FV/(1 + r)^n$, where n = number of years until cash flow, FV = cash flow amount, and r = spot rate.

A is incorrect because the price on the Eurex exchange, €103.7956, was calculated using the yield to maturity rate to discount the cash flows when the spot rates should have been used. C is incorrect because the price on the Frankfurt exchange, €103.7565, uses the Year 3 spot rate to discount all the cash flows.

3. C is correct. Because Node 2–2 is the middle node rate in Year 2, it will be close to the implied one-year forward rate one year from now (as derived from the spot curve). Node 4–1 should be equal to the product of Node 4–5 and $e^{0.8}$. Lastly, Node 3–2 cannot be derived from Node 2–2; it can be derived from any other Year 3 node; for example, Node 3–2 can be derived from Node 3–4 (equal to the product of Node 3–4 and $e^{4\sigma}$).
4. C is correct. The value of a bond at a particular node, in this case Node 1–2, can be derived by working backwards from the two nodes to the right of that node on the tree. In this case, those two nodes are the middle node in Year 2, equal to 104.0168, and the lower node in Year 2, equal to 104.6350. The bond value at Node 1–2 is calculated as follows:

$$\begin{aligned} \text{Value} &= 0.5 \times [(104.0168/1.014925 + 104.6350/1.014925)] + 2.5 \\ &= 0.5 \times [102.4872 + 103.0963] + 2.5 \\ &= 105.2917 \end{aligned}$$

   A is incorrect because the calculation does not include the coupon payment. B is incorrect because the calculation incorrectly uses the Year 0 and Year 1 node values.
5. A is correct. Calibrating a binomial interest rate tree to match a specific term structure is important because we can use the known valuation of a benchmark bond from the spot rate pricing to verify the accuracy of the rates shown in the binomial interest rate tree. Once its accuracy is confirmed, the interest rate tree can then be used to value bonds with embedded options. While discounting with spot rates will produce arbitrage-free valuations for option-free bonds, this spot rate method will not work for bonds with embedded options where expected future cash flows are interest-rate dependent (as rate changes impact the likelihood of options being exercised). The interest rate tree allows for the alternative paths that a bond with embedded options might take.

   B is incorrect because calibration does not identify mispriced benchmark bonds. In fact, benchmark bonds are employed to prove the accuracy of the binomial interest rate tree, as they are assumed to be correctly priced by the market.

   C is incorrect because the calibration of the binomial interest rate tree is designed to produce an arbitrage-free valuation approach and such an approach does not allow a market participant to realize arbitrage profits though stripping and reconstitution.
6. A is correct. Volatility is one of the two key assumptions required to estimate rates for the binomial interest rate tree. Increasing the volatility from 10% to 15% would cause the possible forward rates to spread out on the tree as it increases the exponent in the relationship multiple between nodes ($e^{x\sigma}$, where x = 2 times the number of nodes above the

lowest node in a given year in the interest rate tree). Conversely, using a lower estimate of volatility would cause the forward rates to narrow or converge to the implied forward rates from the prevailing yield curve.

B is incorrect because volatility is a key assumption in the binomial interest rate tree model. Any change in volatility will cause a change in the implied forward rates.

C is incorrect because increasing the volatility from 10% to 15% causes the possible forward rates to spread out on the tree, not converge to the implied forward rates from the current yield curve. Rates will converge to the implied forward rates when lower estimates of volatility are assumed.

7. B is correct. Bond B's arbitrage-free price is calculated as follows:

$$\frac{3}{1.02}+\frac{103}{1.02^2}=101.9416$$

which is higher than the bond's market price of 100.9641. Therefore, an arbitrage opportunity exists. Since the bond's value (100.9641) is less than the sum of the values of its discounted cash flows individually (101.9416), a trader would perceive an arbitrage opportunity and could buy the bond while selling claims to the individual cash flows (zeros), capturing the excess value. The arbitrage-free prices of Bond A and Bond C are equal to the market prices of the respective bonds, so there is no arbitrage opportunity for these two bonds:

Bond A:

$$\frac{1}{1.02}+\frac{101}{1.02^2}=98.0584$$

Bond C:

$$\frac{5}{1.02}+\frac{105}{1.02^2}=105.8247$$

8. C is correct. The first step in the solution is to find the correct spot rate (zero-coupon rates) for each year's cash flow. The benchmark bonds in Exhibit 2 are conveniently priced at par so the yields to maturity and the coupon rates on the bonds are the same. Because the one-year issue has only one cash flow remaining, the YTM equals the spot rate of 3% (or z_1 = 3%). The spot rates for Year 2 (z_2) and Year 3 (z_3) are calculated as follows:

$$100=\frac{4}{1.0300}+\frac{104}{(1+z_2)^2};\ z_2=4.02\%$$

$$100=\frac{5}{1.0300}+\frac{5}{(1.0402)^2}+\frac{105}{(1+z_3)^3};\ z_3=5.07\%$$

The correct arbitrage-free price for the Hutto-Barkley Inc. bond is:

$$P_0=\frac{3}{(1.0300)}+\frac{3}{(1.0402)^2}+\frac{103}{(1.0507)^3}=94.4828$$

Therefore, the bond is mispriced by 94.4828 – 94.9984 = –0.5156 per 100 of par value.

A is incorrect because the correct spot rates are not calculated and instead the Hutto-Barkley Inc. bond is discounted using the respective YTM for each maturity. Therefore, this leads to an incorrect mispricing of 94.6616 – 94.9984 = –0.3368 per 100 of par value.

B is incorrect because the spot rates are derived using the coupon rate for Year 3 (maturity) instead of using each year's respective coupon rate to employ the bootstrap methodology. This leads to an incorrect mispricing of 94.5302 – 94.9984 = –0.4682 per 100 of par value.

9. B is correct. The Luna y Estrellas Intl. bond contains an embedded option. Method 1 will produce an arbitrage-free valuation for option-free bonds; however, for bonds with embedded options, changes in future interest rates impact the likelihood the option will be exercised and so impact future cash flows. Therefore, to develop a framework that values bonds with embedded options, interest rates must be allowed to take on different potential values in the future based on some assumed level of volatility (Method 2).

   A and C are incorrect because the Hutto-Barkley Inc. bond and the Peaton Scorpio Motors bond are both option-free bonds and can be valued using either Method 1 or Method 2 to produce an arbitrage-free valuation.

10. B is correct. The first step is to identify the cash flows:

Time 0	Time 1	Time 2	Time 3
			106
		6	
	6		106
0		6	
	6		106
		6	
			106

Next, calculate the cash flows for each year beginning with Year 3 and move backwards to Year 1:

Year 3:

$$0.5\times\left[\left(\frac{106}{1.06}\right)+\left(\frac{106}{1.06}\right)\right]+6=106.0000$$

$$0.5\times\left[\left(\frac{106}{1.05}\right)+\left(\frac{106}{1.05}\right)\right]+6=106.9524$$

$$0.5\times\left[\left(\frac{106}{1.03}\right)+\left(\frac{106}{1.03}\right)\right]+6=108.9126$$

Year 2:

$$0.5\times\left[\left(\frac{106.0000}{1.04}\right)+\left(\frac{106.9524}{1.04}\right)\right]+6=108.3810$$

$$0.5\times\left[\left(\frac{106.9524}{1.02}\right)+\left(\frac{108.9126}{1.02}\right)\right]+6=111.8162$$

Year 1:

$$0.5\times\left[\left(\frac{108.3810}{1.01}\right)+\left(\frac{111.8162}{1.01}\right)\right]=109.0085$$

A is incorrect because the coupon payment is not accounted for at each node calculation. C is incorrect because it assumes that a coupon is paid in Year 1 (time zero) when no coupon payment is paid at time zero.

CHAPTER 9

VALUATION AND ANALYSIS: BONDS WITH EMBEDDED OPTIONS

SOLUTIONS

1. C is correct. The call option embedded in Bond #2 can be exercised only at two predetermined dates: 1 October 20X1 and 1 October 20X2. Thus, the call feature is Bermudan style.
2. C is correct. The bond that would most likely protect investors against a significant increase in interest rates is the putable bond, i.e., Bond #3. When interest rates have risen and higher-yield bonds are available, a put option allows the bondholders to put back the bonds to the issuer prior to maturity and to reinvest the proceeds of the retired bonds in higher-yielding bonds.
3. B is correct. A fall in interest rates results in a rise in bond values. For a callable bond such as Bond #2, the upside potential is capped because the issuer is more likely to call the bond. In contrast, the upside potential for a putable bond such as Bond #3 is uncapped. Thus, a fall in interest rates would result in a putable bond having more upside potential than an otherwise identical callable bond. Note that A is incorrect because the effective duration of a putable bond increases, not decreases, with a fall in interest rates—the bond is less likely to be put and thus behaves more like an option-free bond. C is also incorrect because the effective convexity of a putable bond is always positive. It is the effective convexity of a callable bond that will change from positive to negative if interest rates fall and the call option is near the money.

4. A is correct:

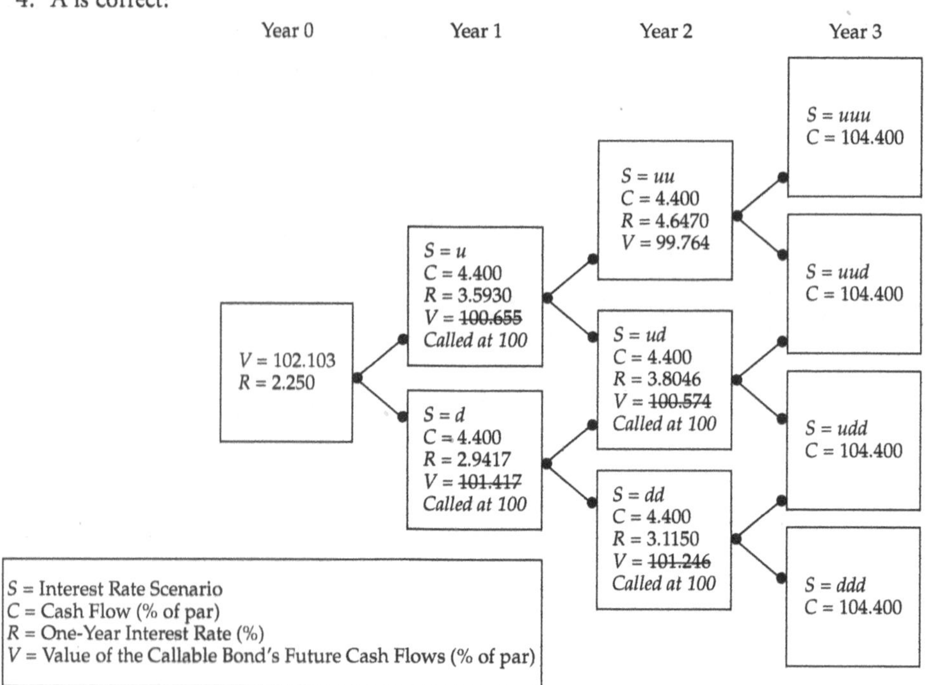

5. C is correct:

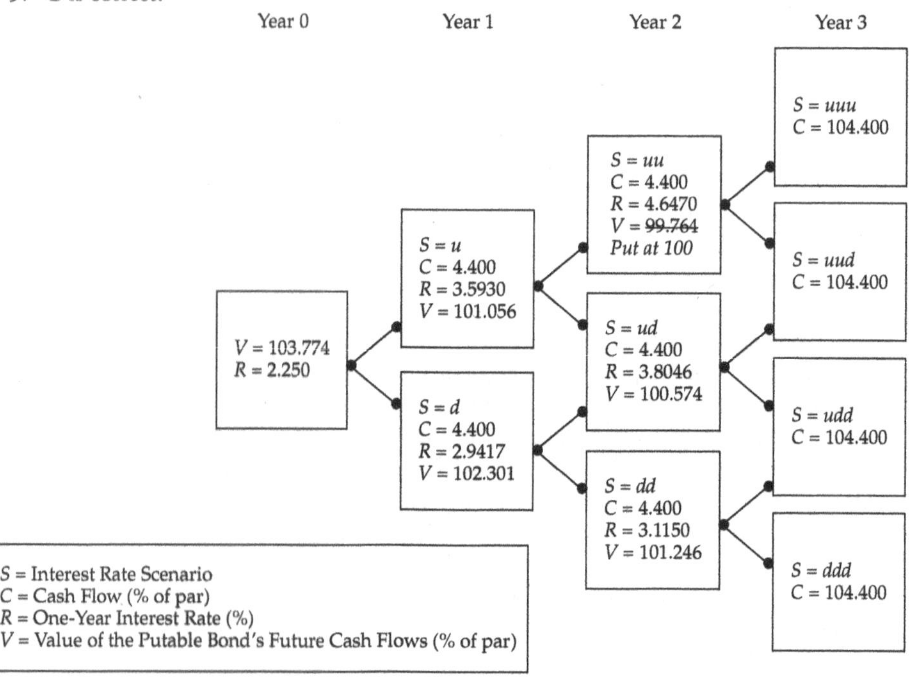

6. C is correct. Bond #3 is a putable bond, and the value of a put option increases as interest rates rise. At higher interest rates, the value of the underlying option-free bond (straight bond) declines, but the decline is offset partially by the increase in the value of the embedded put option, which is more likely to be exercised.
7. C is correct. Regardless of the type of option, an increase in interest rate volatility results in an increase in option value. Because the value of a putable bond is equal to the value of the straight bond *plus* the value of the embedded put option, Bond #3 will increase in value if interest rate volatility increases. Put another way, an increase in interest rate volatility will most likely result in more scenarios where the put option is exercised, which increases the values calculated in the interest rate tree and, thus, the value of the putable bond.
8. C is correct. Bond #2 is a callable bond, and the value of the embedded call option increases as the yield curve flattens. When the yield curve is upward sloping, the one-period forward rates on the interest rate tree are high and opportunities for the issuer to call the bond are fewer. When the yield curve flattens or inverts, many nodes on the tree have lower forward rates, which increases the opportunities to call and, thus, the value of the embedded call option.
9. B is correct. The conversion price of a convertible bond is equal to the par value divided by the conversion ratio—that is, \$1,000/31= \$32.26 per share.
10. B is correct. The market price on 19 October 20X0 (\$37.50) is above the conversion price of \$1,000/31 = \$32.26 per share. Thus, the convertible bond exhibits mostly stock risk-return characteristics, and a fall in the stock price will result in a fall in the convertible bond price. However, the change in the convertible bond price is less than the change in the stock price because the convertible bond has a floor—that floor is the value of the straight bond.
11. C is correct. The option-adjusted spread (OAS) is the constant spread added to all the one-period forward rates that makes the arbitrage-free value of a risky bond equal to its market price. The OAS approach is often used to assess bond relative values. If two bonds have the same characteristics and credit quality, they should have the same OAS. If this is not the case, the bond with the largest OAS (i.e., Bond #2) is likely to be underpriced (cheap) relative to the bond with the smallest OAS (Bond #1).
12. A is correct. The effective duration of a floating-rate bond is close to the time to next reset. As the reset for Bond #6 is annual, the effective duration of this bond is lower than or equal to 1.
13. B is correct. Effective duration indicates the sensitivity of a bond's price to a 100 bps parallel shift of the benchmark yield curve assuming no change in the bond's credit spread. The effective duration of an option-free bond such as Bond #3 changes very little in response to interest rate movements. As interest rates rise, a call option moves out of the money, which increases the value of the callable bond and lengthens its effective duration. In contrast, as interest rates rise, a put option moves into the money, which limits the price depreciation of the putable bond and shortens its effective duration. Thus, the bond whose effective duration will lengthen if interest rates rise is the callable bond, i.e., Bond #4.
14. B is correct. The effective duration of Bond #4 can be calculated using Equation 3 from the reading, where ΔCurve is 20 bps, PV_- is 101.238, and PV_+ is 100.478. PV_0, the current full price of the bond (i.e., with no shift), is not given but it can be calculated using Exhibit 3 as follows:

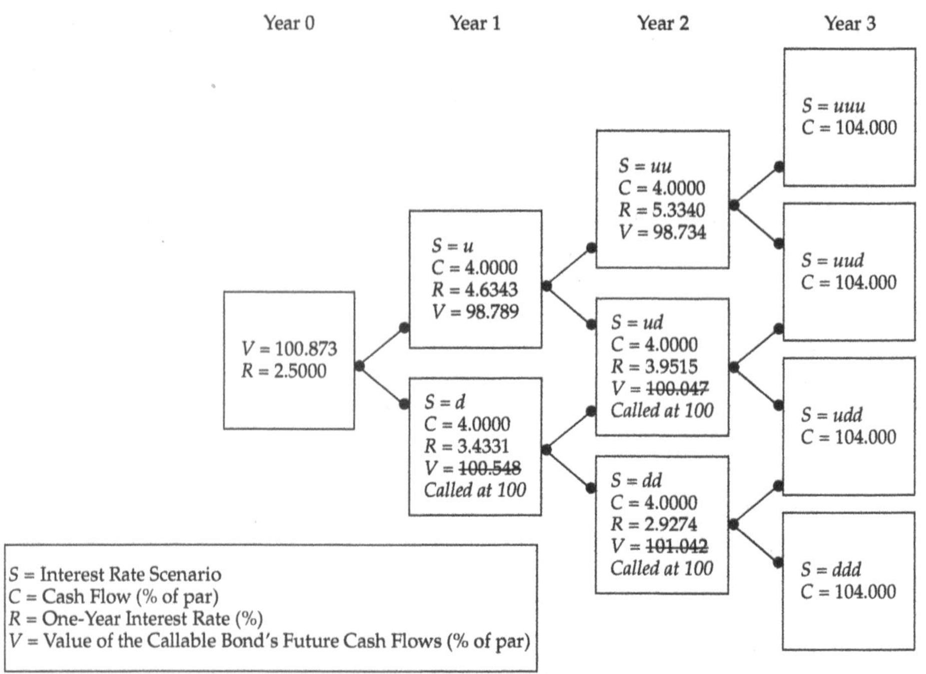

Thus, the effective duration of Bond #4 is:

$$\text{Effective duration} = \frac{101.238 - 100.478}{2 \times (0.0020) \times (100.873)} = 1.88$$

15. A is correct:

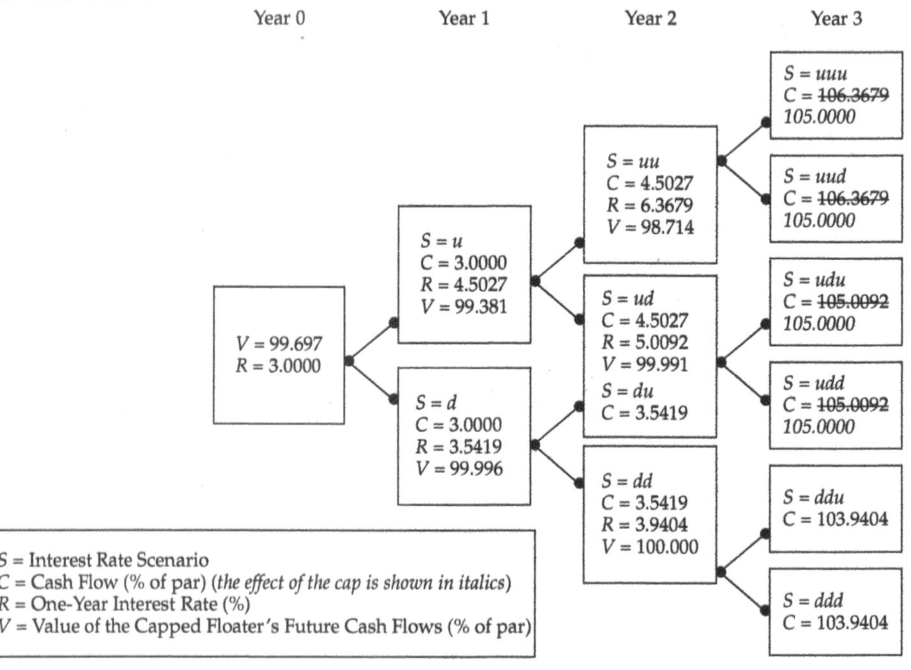

16. C is correct:

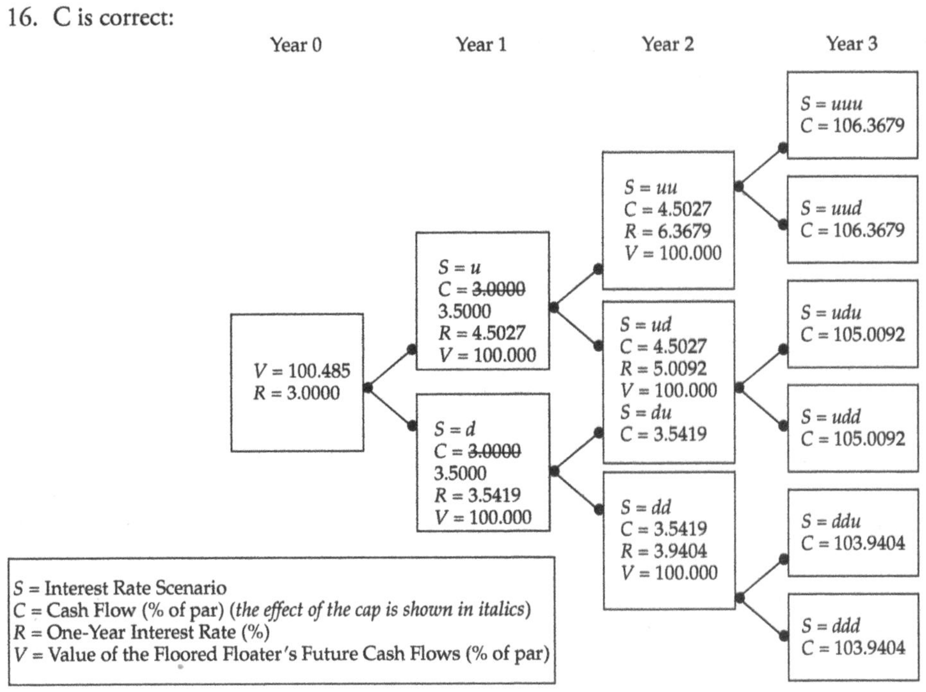

17. B is correct. A convertible bond includes a conversion option, which is a call option on the issuer's common stock. This conversion option gives the bondholders the right to convert their debt into equity. Thus, the value of Bond #9, the convertible bond, is equal to the value of Bond #10, the underlying option-free bond (straight bond), plus the value of a call option on Whorton's common stock.
18. A is correct. The minimum value of a convertible bond is equal to the greater of the conversion value of the convertible bond (i.e., Bond #9) and the current value of the straight bond (i.e., Bond #10).
19. C is correct. The risk-return characteristics of a convertible bond depend on the market price of the issuer's common stock (underlying share price) relative to the bond's conversion price. When the underlying share price is well below the conversion price, the convertible bond exhibits mostly bond risk-return characteristics. In this case, the price of the convertible bond is mainly affected by interest rate movements and the issuer's credit spreads. In contrast, when the underlying share price is above the conversion price, the convertible bond exhibits mostly stock risk-return characteristics. In this case, the price of the convertible bond is mainly affected by the issuer's common stock price movements. The underlying share price ($30) is lower than the conversion price of Bond #9 ($50). Thus, Bond #9 exhibits mostly bond risk-return characteristics and is least affected by Whorton's common stock price movements.

CHAPTER 10

THE TERM STRUCTURE AND INTEREST RATE DYNAMICS

SOLUTIONS

1. Three forward rates can be calculated from the one-, two-, and three-year spot rates. The rate on a one-year loan that begins at the end of Year 1 can be calculated using the one- and two-year spot rates; in the following equation one would solve for $f(1,1)$:

$$[1 + r(2)]^2 = [1 + r(1)]^1[1 + f(1,1)]^1$$

   The rate on a one-year loan that starts at the end of Year 2 can be calculated from the two- and three-year spot rates; in the following equation one would solve for $f(2,1)$:

$$[1 + r(3)]^3 = [1 + r(2)]^2[1 + f(2,1)]^1$$

   Additionally, the rate on a two-year loan that begins at the end of Year 1 can be computed from the one- and three-year spot rates; in the following equation one would solve for $f(1,2)$:

$$[1 + r(3)]^3 = [1 + r(1)]^1[1 + f(1,2)]^2$$

2. For the two-year forward rate one year from now of 2%, the two interpretations are as follows:
   - 2% is the rate that will make an investor indifferent between buying a three-year zero-coupon bond or investing in a one-year zero-coupon bond and when it matures reinvesting in a zero-coupon bond that matures in two years.
   - 2% is the rate that can be locked in today by buying a three-year zero-coupon bond rather than investing in a one-year zero-coupon bond and when it matures reinvesting in a zero-coupon bond that matures in two years.
3. A flat yield curve implies that all spot interest rates are the same. When the spot rate is the same for every maturity, successive applications of the forward rate model will show that all the forward rates will also be the same and equal to the spot rate.

4. A. The yield to maturity of a coupon bond is the expected rate of return on a bond if the bond is held to maturity, there is no default, and the bond and all coupons are reinvested at the original yield to maturity.
   B. Yes, it is possible. For example, if reinvestment rates for the future coupons are lower than the initial yield to maturity, a bond holder may experience lower realized returns.
5. If forward rates are higher than expected future spot rates, the market price of the bond will be higher than the intrinsic value. This is because, everything else held constant, the market is currently discounting the bond's cash flows at a higher rate than the investor's expected future spot rates. The investor can capitalize on this by purchasing the undervalued bond. If expected future spot rates are realized, then bond prices should rise, thus generating gains for the investor.
6. The strategy of riding the yield curve is one in which a bond trader attempts to generate a total return over a given investment horizon that exceeds the return to bond with maturity matched to the horizon. The strategy involves buying a bond with maturity more distant than the investment horizon. Assuming an upward sloping yield curve, if the yield curve does not change level or shape, as the bond approaches maturity (or rolls down the yield curve) it will be priced at successively lower yields. So, as long as the bond is held for a period less than maturity, it should generate higher returns because of price gains.
7. Some countries do not have active government bond markets with trading at all maturities. For those countries without a liquid government bond market but with an active swap market, there are typically more points available to construct a swap curve than a government bond yield curve. For those markets, the swap curve may be a superior benchmark.
8. The Z-spread is the constant basis point spread added to the default-free spot curve to correctly price a risky bond. A Z-spread of 100 bps for a particular bond would imply that adding a fixed spread of 100 bps to the points along the spot yield curve will correctly price the bond. A higher Z-spread would imply a riskier bond.
9. The TED spread is the difference between a Libor rate and the US T-Bill rate of matching maturity. It is an indicator of perceived credit risk in the general economy. In particular, because sovereign debt instruments are typically the benchmark for the lowest default risk instruments in a given market, and loans between banks (often at Libor) have some counterparty risk, the TED spread is considered to at least in part reflect default (or counterparty) risk in the banking sector.
10. The local expectations theory asserts that the total return over a one-month horizon for a five-year zero-coupon bond would be the same as for a two-year zero-coupon bond.
11. Both theories attempt to explain the shape of any yield curve in terms of supply and demand for bonds. In segmented market theory, bond market participants are limited to purchase of maturities that match the timing of their liabilities. In the preferred habitat theory, participants have a preferred maturity for asset purchases, but may deviate from it if they feel returns in other maturities offer sufficient compensation for leaving their preferred maturity segment.
12. A. Studies have shown that there have been three factors that affect Treasury returns: (1) changes in the level of the yield curve, (2) changes in the slope of the yield curve, and (3) changes in the curvature of the yield curve. Changes in the level refer to upward or downward shifts in the yield curve. For example, an upward shift in the yield curve is likely to result in lower returns across all maturities. Changes in the slope of the yield curve relate to the steepness of the yield curve. Thus, if the yield curve steepens it is likely to result in higher returns for short maturity bonds and lower returns

for long maturity bonds. An example of a change in the curvature of the yield curve is a situation where rates fall at the short and long end of the yield curve while rising for intermediate maturities. In this situation returns on short and long maturities are likely to rise while declining for intermediate maturity bonds.

B. Empirically, the most important factor is the change in the level of interest rates.

C. Key rate durations and a measure based on sensitivities to level, slope, and curvature movements can address shaping risk, but effective duration cannot.

13. C is correct. There is no spot rate information to provide rates for a loan that terminates in five years. That is, $f(2,3)$ is calculated as follows:

$$f(2,3)=\sqrt[3]{\frac{[1+r(5)]^5}{[1+r(2)]^2}}$$

The equation above indicates that in order to calculate the rate for a three-year loan beginning at the end of two years you need the five-year spot rate $r(5)$ and the two-year spot rate $r(2)$. However $r(5)$ is not provided.

14. A is correct. The forward rate for a one-year loan beginning in one year $f(1,1)$ is $1.04^2/1.03 - 1 = 5\%$. The rate for a one-year loan beginning in two years $f(2,1)$ is $1.05^3/1.04^2 - 1 = 7\%$. This confirms that an upward-sloping yield curve is consistent with an upward-sloping forward curve.

15. C is correct. If one-period forward rates are decreasing with maturity then the forward curve is downward sloping. This turn implies a downward sloping yield curve where longer term spot rates $r(T+T^*)$ are less than shorter term spot rates $r(T)$.

16. C is correct. From the forward rate model, we have

$$[1+r(2)]^2 = [1+r(1)]^1[1+f(1,1)]^1$$

Using the one- and two-year spot rates, we have

$$(1+.05)^2 = (1+.04)^1[1+f(1,1)]^1,\text{ so } \frac{(1+.05)^2}{(1+.04)^1}-1 = f(1,1) = 6.010\%$$

17. C is correct. From the forward rate model,

$$[1+r(3)]^3 = [1+r(1)]^1[1+f(1,2)]^2$$

Using the one-and three-year spot rates, we find

$$(1+0.06)^3 = (1+0.04)^1[1+f(1,2)]^2,\text{ so } \sqrt{\frac{(1+0.06)^3}{(1+0.04)^1}}-1 = f(1,2) = 7.014\%$$

18. C is correct. From the forward rate model,

$$[1+r(3)]^3 = [1+r(2)]^2[1+f(2,1)]^1$$

Using the two-and three-year spot rates, we find

$$(1+0.06)^3 = (1+0.05)^2[1+f(2,1)]^1,\text{ so } \frac{(1+0.06)^3}{(1+0.05)^2}-1 = f(2,1) = 8.029\%$$

19. A is correct. We can convert spot rates to spot prices to find $P(3) = \frac{1}{(1.06)^3} = 0.8396$. The forward pricing model can be used to find the price of the five-year zero as $P(T^*+T) = P(T^*)F(T^*,T)$, so $P(5) = P(3)F(3,2) = 0.8396 \times 0.8479 = 0.7119$.

20. B is correct. Applying the forward rate model, we find

$$[1 + r(3)]^3 = [1 + r(1)]^1[1 + f(1,1)]^1[1 + f(2,1)]^1$$

$$\text{So } [1 + r(3)]^3 = (1 + 0.04)^1(1 + 0.06)^1(1 + 0.08)^1, \sqrt[3]{1.1906} - 1 = r(3) = 5.987\%.$$

21. B is correct. We can convert spot rates to spot prices and use the forward pricing model, so $P(1) = \frac{1}{(1.05)^1} = 0.9524$. The forward pricing model is $P(T^* + T) = P(T^*)F(T^*, T)$ so $P(2) = P(1)F(1,1) = 0.9524 \times 0.9346 = 0.8901$.
22. A is correct. The swap rate is the interest rate for the fixed-rate leg of an interest rate swap.
23. A is correct. The swap spread = 1.00% - 0.63% = 0.37% or 37 bps.
24. C is correct. The fixed leg of the five-year fixed-for-floating swap will be equal to the five-year Treasury rate plus the swap spread: 2% + 0.5% = 2.5%.
25. A is correct. The TED spread is the difference between the three-month Libor rate and the three-month Treasury bill rate. If the T-bill rate falls and Libor does not change, the TED spread will increase.
26. A is correct. The Z-spread is the single rate which, when added to the rates of the spot yield curve, will provide the correct discount rates to price a particular risky bond.
27. A is correct. The 200 bps Z-spread can be added to the 5% rates from the yield curve to price the bond. The resulting 7% discount rate will be the same for all of the bond's cash-flows, since the yield curve is flat. A 7% coupon bond yielding 7% will be priced at par.
28. B is correct. The higher Z-spread for Bond B implies it is riskier than Bond A. The higher discount rate will make the price of Bond B lower than Bond A.
29. A is correct. The Ho–Lee model is arbitrage-free and can be calibrated to closely match the observed term structure.

CHAPTER 11

FIXED-INCOME PORTFOLIO MANAGEMENT—PART I

SOLUTIONS

1. The tracking risk is the standard deviation of the active returns. For the data shown in the problem, the tracking risk is 28.284 bps, as shown below:

Period	Portfolio Return	Benchmark Return	Active Return	(AR – Avg. AR)^2
1	14.10%	13.70%	0.400%	0.00090%
2	8.20	8.00	0.200	0.00010
3	7.80	8.00	-0.200	0.00090
4	3.20	3.50	-0.300	0.00160
5	2.60	2.40	0.200	0.00010
6	3.30	3.00	0.300	0.00040
Average active return per period =			0.100%	
Sum of the squared deviations =				0.00400%
Tracking risk (std. dev.) =				0.28284%

2. The portfolio is more sensitive to changes in the spread because its spread duration is 3.151 compared with the benchmark's 2.834. The portfolio's higher spread duration is primarily a result of the portfolio's greater weight on agency securities. The spread duration for each can be calculated by taking a weighted average of the individual sectors' durations. Because there is a difference between the portfolio's and the benchmark's spread duration, the tracking risk will be higher than if the two were more closely matched.

Sector	Portfolio % of Portfolio	Portfolio Spread Duration	Portfolio Contribution to Spread Duration	Benchmark % of Portfolio	Benchmark Spread Duration	Benchmark Contribution to Spread Duration
Treasury	22.70	0.00	0.000	23.10	0.00	0.000
Agencies	12.20	4.56	0.556	6.54	4.41	0.288
Financial institutions	6.23	3.23	0.201	5.89	3.35	0.197
Industrials	14.12	11.04	1.559	14.33	10.63	1.523
Utilities	6.49	2.10	0.136	6.28	2.58	0.162
Non-US credit	6.56	2.05	0.134	6.80	1.98	0.135
Mortgage	31.70	1.78	0.564	33.20	1.11	0.369
Asset backed	—	2.40	0.000	1.57	3.34	0.052
CMBS	—	5.60	0.000	2.29	4.67	0.107
Total	100.00		3.151	100.00		2.834

3. Dollar duration is a measure of the change in portfolio value for a 100 bps change in market yields. It is defined as

$$\text{Dollar duration} = \text{Duration} \times \text{Dollar value} \times 0.01$$

A. A portfolio's dollar duration is the sum of the dollar durations of the component securities. The dollar duration of this portfolio at the beginning of the period is $162,636, which is calculated as

Security	Initial Values: Price	Market Value	Duration	Dollar Duration
Bond #1	$106.110	$1,060,531	5.909	$ 62,667
Bond #2	98.200	981,686	3.691	36,234
Bond #3	109.140	1,090,797	5.843	63,735
		Portfolio dollar duration =		$162,636

At the end of one year, the portfolio's dollar duration has changed to $136,318, as shown below.

Security	After 1 Year: Price	Market Value	Duration	Dollar Duration
Bond #1	$104.240	$1,042,043	5.177	$ 53,947
Bond #2	98.084	980,461	2.817	27,620
Bond #3	106.931	1,068,319	5.125	54,751
		Portfolio dollar duration =		$136,318

B. The rebalancing ratio is a ratio of the original dollar duration to the new dollar duration:

$$\text{Rebalancing ratio} = \$162{,}636/\$136{,}318 = 1.193$$

C. The portfolio requires each position to be increased by 19.3 percent. The cash required for this rebalancing is calculated as:

$$\begin{aligned}\text{Cash required} &= 0.193 \times (\$1{,}042{,}043 + 980{,}461 + 1{,}068{,}319)\\ &= \$596{,}529\end{aligned}$$

4. B is correct. Portfolio duration is a weighted average of the component durations. In this problem, $(0.4774 \times 5.50) + (0.1479 \times 5.80) + (0.1235 \times 4.50) + (0.2512 \times 4.65) = 5.20735$. Round to 5.21.
5. A is correct. Spread duration is a measure of a non-Treasury security's price change as a result of a change in the spread between the security and a Treasury. The portfolio spread duration is the weighted average duration of those securities in the portfolio that have a yield above the default-free yield (i.e., non-Treasuries). In this problem, the agencies, corporates, and mortgage-backed securities have a spread. Using their original weights in the portfolio, the spread duration is $(0.1479 \times 5.80) + (0.1235 \times 4.50) + (0.2512 \times 4.65) = 2.58165$. Round to 2.58.
6. C is correct. Exhibit 1 makes clear that the portfolio weights differ and for some sectors quite dramatically from those of the index and that the durations of the portfolio components differ from their respective durations in the index. Thus the manager is using active management because he had both duration and sector mismatches and not on a small scale.
7. B is correct. The market capitalization of the bond universe is large—much larger than that for equities. Alonso is incorrect in identifying this as a limiting factor. Information (data) for the other two factors can be impossible to acquire.
8. B is correct. Calculate the holding period return for the Treasury 4.125% 15 May 2011 by using the current price of 100.40625 (Exhibit 2), Alonso's forecast of 99.50, and a semi-annual coupon of 2.0625. The problem informs that there is zero accrued interest. The 6-month total return is $(99.50 + 2.0625 - 100.40625)/100.40625 = 1.15\%$.
9. A is correct. Alonso is not simply going to reinvest the entire proceeds of the sale into 10-year Treasuries because his stated desire is to maintain the dollar duration of the portfolio. The sale price of $10 million par value of the 5-year bond is found by multiplying $\$10{,}000{,}000 \times 1.0040625 = \$10{,}040{,}625$. The dollar duration of the 5-year is $4.53 \times \$10{,}040{,}625 \times 0.01 = \$454{,}840.31$. Now divide $454,840.31 by the product of the duration of the 10-year and its quoted price and 0.01 to get the par value of the 10-year. The result is $\$454{,}840.31/(8.22 \times 1.0909375 \times 0.01) = \$5{,}072{,}094$.
10. B is correct. Chow's statement #1 is incorrect because what she describes does not remove all risks. Credit risk destroys the immunization match; therefore, the statement is incorrect. The risk to immunization comes from non-parallel shifts in the yield curve.
11. C is correct. Portfolio A is a zero-coupon bond and thus has no reinvestment rate risk. Portfolio B has lower dispersion in maturities than Portfolio C. Therefore, Portfolio C has more reinvestment rate risk than Portfolio B.
12. B is correct. The SRB will accept (i.e., require) a return of 4.50% (semiannual compounding). Find the time ten future value of $100 million at this rate. The answer is $\$100{,}000{,}000 \times (1 + .045/2)^{20} = \$156{,}050{,}920$.
13. A is correct. Haley's statement #1 defines the risk-costs tradeoffs of cash flow matching versus multiple liabilities immunization.

14. C is correct. If the distribution of the durations of the assets is wider than that of the liabilities, the durations of the assets after a parallel yield curve shift (whether up or down) will envelope the durations of the liabilities after the shift. The immunization can be maintained, although rebalancing may be necessary.
15. C is correct. Horizon matching creates a duration-matched portfolio with the added constraint that it be cash-flow-matched in the first few years. Cash flow matching the initial portion of the liability stream reduces the risk associated with nonparallel shifts of the yield curve.

CHAPTER 12

FIXED-INCOME PORTFOLIO MANAGEMENT—PART II

SOLUTIONS

1. A. Because you are considering bonds with embedded options, the returns of portfolios are unlikely to be normally distributed. Because shortfall risk is not based on normality assumption, however, it may be used as a risk measure. Furthermore, because the client has specified a minimum target return (£25,000/£2,000,000 or 1.25 percent over the next six months), shortfall risk could be a useful measure to look at.

   B. One of the shortcomings of shortfall risk is that it is not as commonly used as standard deviation, and there is relatively less familiarity with shortfall risk. Also, its statistical properties are not well known. Unlike VAR, it does not take the form of a dollar amount. Finally, the shortfall risk gives the probability of the returns from the portfolio falling below the specified minimum target return, but it does not provide any information about the extent to which the return may be below the specified minimum target.

2. A. Because the fund desires to increase the duration, it would need to buy futures contracts.

   B. D_T = target duration for the portfolio = 10
   D_I = initial duration for the portfolio = 8.17
   P_I = initial market value of the portfolio = €75 million
   D_{CTD} = the duration of the cheapest-to-deliver bond = 9.35
   P_{CTD} = the price of the cheapest-to-deliver bond = €130,000
   Conversion factor for the cheapest-to-deliver bond = 1.06

$$\text{Approximate number of contracts} = \frac{(D_T - D_I)P_I}{D_{CTD}P_{CTD}} \times \text{Conversion factor for the CTD bond}$$

$$= \frac{(10.0 - 8.17) \times 75{,}000{,}000}{9.35 \times 130{,}000} \times 1.06 = 119.69$$

Thus, the pension fund would need to buy 119 futures contracts to achieve the desired increase in duration.

3. Covered call writing is a good strategy if the rates are not going to change much from their present level. The sale of the calls brings in premium income that provides partial protection in case rates increase. The additional income from writing calls can be used to offset declining prices. If rates fall, portfolio appreciation is limited because the short call position is a liability for the seller, and this liability increases as rates go down. Consequently, there is limited upside potential for the covered call writer. Overall, this drawback does not have negative consequences if rates do not change because the added income from the sale of calls would be obtained without sacrificing any gains. Thus, Consultant A, who suggested selling covered calls, probably believes that the interest rates would not change much in either direction.

   Doing nothing would be a good strategy for a bondholder if he believes that rates are going down. The bondholder could simply gain from the increasing bond prices. Thus, Consultant B, who suggested doing nothing, likely believes that the interest rates would go down.

   If one has no clear opinion about the interest rate outlook but would like to avoid risk, selling interest rate futures would be a good strategy. If interest rates were to increase, the loss in value of bonds would be offset by the gains from futures. Thus, Consultant C, who suggested selling interest rate futures, is likely the one who has no opinion.

   Paying the premium for buying the puts would not be a bad idea if a bondholder believes that interest rates are going to increase. Thus, Consultant D is likely the one who believes that the interest rates are headed upward.

4. The payoff to More Money Funds would be:

   $$\text{Payoff} = (0.030 - \text{Credit spread at maturity}) \times \$10 \text{ million} \times 5$$

   A. Payoff = $(0.030 - 0.025) \times \$10$ million $\times 5 = \$250{,}000$.
   B. Payoff = $(0.030 - 0.035) \times \$10$ million $\times 5 = \$250{,}000$, or a loss of \$250,000.
   C. The maximum gain would be in the unlikely event of credit spread at the forward contract maturity being zero. So, the best possible payoff is $(0.030 - 0.000) \times \$10$ million $\times 5 = \$1{,}500{,}000$.

5. First, let us compute the amount in each of the three tranches in the CDO. The senior tranche is 70 percent of \$250 million = \$175 million. The junior tranche is 20 percent of \$250 million = \$50 million. The rest is the equity tranche = \$250 million − \$175 million − \$50 million = \$25 million.

   Now let us compute the amount that would be received by the equity tranche. Annual interest generated by the collateral would be 6 + 5 = 11 percent of \$250 million = \$27.5 million. Annual interest received by the senior tranche would be 7.5 + 0.5 = 8 percent of \$175 million = \$14 million. Annual interest received by the junior tranche would be 6 + 3 = 9 percent of \$50 million = \$4.5 million. So, the amount to be received by the equity tranche is 27.5 − 14 − 4.5 = \$9 million. This amount represents a return of 9/25 = 0.36 or 36 percent.

6. The mispricing occurs because the forward rate doesn't conform to the covered interest rate parity theorem.

   A. The current discount rate is −2.48 percent [i.e., (\$1.18 − \$1.21)/\$1.21].
   B. The covered interest rate parity theorem states that the forward foreign exchange rate for a fixed period must be equal to the interest rate differentials between the two countries.

   $$\text{Forward rate} = \text{Spot rate} \times (1 + \text{Domestic interest rate}) \,/\, (1 + \text{Foreign interest rate})$$

Substituting into the formula:

$$\text{Forward rate} = \$1.21(1 + 0.02)/(1 + 0.03)$$
$$\text{Forward rate} = \$1.198$$

7. The investor can evaluate the change in value of the Canadian bond if US rates change by 80 bps as follows:

   Δ in value of Canadian bond = Candian bond's duration $\times$ Canada country beta $\times\,\Delta$ in US rates
   Δ in value of Canadian bond = $8.40 \times 0.63 \times 0.80$ percent
   Δ in value of Canadian bond = 4.23 percent

8. Let *W* denote the spread widening.

   $$\text{Change in price} = \text{Duration} \times \text{Change in yield}$$
   $$\text{Change in price} = 8.3 \times W$$

   Assuming the increase in price caused by the spread widening will be 0.75 percent

   $$0.75 \text{ percent} = 8.3 \times W$$

   Solving for the spread widening, *W*,

   $$W = 0.0904 \text{ percent} = 9.04 \text{ bps}$$

   Thus, a spread widening of 9.04 bps would wipe out the additional yield gained from investing in the US bond. The 0.0904 percent change in rates would wipe out the quarterly yield advantage of 75 bps.
9. The forward premium on the Japanese yen is 2.7 - 1.6 = 1.1 percent. So, the portfolio manager should hedge using a forward contract if the anticipated return on yen is less than 1.1 percent.
   A. Because the anticipated return on yen of 1.5 percent is greater than 1.1 percent, the portfolio manager should not hedge.
   B. Because the anticipated return on yen of 0.5 percent is less than 1.1 percent, the portfolio manager should hedge.
10. The interest rate differential between the UK pound and the US dollar is 4.7 - 4.0 = 0.7 percent. Because this differential is greater than the 0.4 percent return on the US dollar expected by the fund manager, the forward hedged position has a higher expected return than the unhedged position.
11. C is correct. TBW is most likely forecasting a decrease in interest rates based on the desire to take on additional interest rate risks. Based on the recommendation to adjust the average duration across the portfolio, rather than key rate duration adjustments, it conveys the expectation of a parallel yield curve shift.
12. B is correct. Because Ibahn wants to take on additional interest rate risk in the portfolio, she would extend duration. To extend duration, Ibahn would need to purchase interest rate futures contracts.
13. B is correct. The 2-year term leverage would shorten the total duration of the levered portfolio relative to overnight repo by the dollar duration of the 2-year liability. The levered portfolio duration would be longer using overnight repo because its proceeds are being invested in bonds to have the same duration as the unlevered portfolio—thus the net effect is a longer duration because the overnight repo duration is zero.

14. B is correct. The duration of the sample leveraged portfolio = (Total dollar duration/ Investors' equity in the original portfolio) × 100 = ($5,125,000/100,000,000) × 100 = 5.13.
15. A is correct. The cost of a repo on special collateral is actually lower than the standard cost of a repo because those needing that collateral are willing to lend funds at a lower cost to obtain that "special" collateral. The illiquidity of the collateral actually increases the margin requirement for the repo as those lending funds want more margin to offset the risk of them having to liquidate the collateral in the event of a borrower default (the entity using the repo to obtain the funds).
16. C is correct. The effect of leverage on a portfolio is that the distribution of returns widens, both to the upside and the downside. In this case, the cost of carry versus the yield on the portfolio causes the return on the levered portfolio to be lower than the return on the unlevered portfolio when interest rates are unchanged.
17. A is correct. Scenario analysis can help evaluate the contribution of individual assumptions (inputs, like the reinvestment rate assumption) to the total return computation. Also, the distribution of outcomes from a scenario analysis may be so wide that it exceeds a client's risk tolerance, even if the expected return is acceptable.
18. C is correct.

	Borrowed Funds	Equity Funds
Amount Invested	$5,000,000	$2,000,000
Rate of Return (0.30% increase in value)	$15,000	$6,000
Less Interest expense at 4.2% (4.2/12 = 0.35% per 30 day)	$17,500	
Net Profitability	-$2,500	$6,000
Rate of Return on Each Component	-0.05% (–2,500/5,000,000)	0.30%
Rate of Return	0.175% [(–2,500 + 6,000)/2,000,000]	

19. A is correct. The quality of the collateral affects the repo rate. Short sellers' needs can affect the demand/availability of the collateral, and hence the repo rate, when the lender of the funds needs the collateral for a short sale.
20. B is correct. The hedged return is equal to the sum of the domestic risk-free interest rate i_d plus the bond's local risk premium of the foreign bond $r_l - i_f$. The local risk premium of 0.70% on the Japanese bond (1.67 – 0.97) is higher than the local risk premium in any of the other countries.
21. B is correct. The unhedged return is approximately equal to the foreign bond return in local currency terms plus the currency return, which is the percentage change in the spot exchange rate stated in terms of home currency per unit of foreign currency. The expected unhedged return on the German bond is the bond yield of 4.36% plus the expected local currency appreciation of 0.95%, for a total of 5.31%.
22. B is correct. The spread widening equals the additional yield income per quarter (4.62 – 1.67)/4 = 0.7375% for Japan, divided by the higher of the two countries' durations, that is, 73.75/9.12 = 8.09.
23. A is correct. Given the mismatch in the liability and the benchmark they are running against, a flattening of the yield curve would cause the liability to increase faster than the asset.

24. A is correct. Contingent immunization does utilize the entire portfolio for active management.
25. C is correct. Value at risk does not indicate the magnitude of the very worst possible outcomes.
26. C is correct. (5.6 - 6.2) × 3,062,000,000/8.2/100,000 × 1.1 = –2,465, or sell 2,465 contracts.
27. A is correct. Cap risk, interest rate risk, and contingent claim risk are all risks the portfolio manager faces.
28. B is correct. A five-year zero-coupon bond best matches the liability of five years.
29. A. Equity = E = 40 percent of €5 million = €2 million

    Borrowed funds = B = 60 percent of €5 million = €3 million

    k = Cost of borrowed funds = 4.6 percent per year = 4.6/12 or 0.3833 percent per 30 days

    r_F = Return on funds invested = 0.5 percent

    Therefore,

    $$R_E = \text{Return on equity} = r_F = 0.5 \text{ percent}$$
    $$R_B = \text{Return on borrowed funds} = r_F - k = 0.5 - 0.3833 = 0.1167 \text{ percent}$$

    B. R_P = Portfolio rate of return = (Profit on borrowed funds + Profit on equity)/Amount of equity = $[B \times (r_F - k) + E \times r_F]/E$ = [€3 million × (0.5 - 0.3833) + €2 million × 0.5]/€2 million = 0.6750 percent.

    C. R_P = Portfolio rate of return = (Profit on borrowed funds + Profit on equity)/Amount of equity = $[B \times (r_F - k) + E \times r_F]/E$ = [€3 million × (0.3 - 0.3833) + €2 million × 0.3]/€2 million = 0.1751 percent.

    D. If the return on funds invested exceeds the cost of borrowing, then leverage magnifies the portfolio rate of return. This condition holds for the case in Part B, where the return on funds of 0.5 percent exceeds the cost of borrowing of 0.3833 percent, and therefore, the portfolio return (0.6750 percent) is greater than the return on funds.

    If the return on funds invested is less than the cost of borrowing, then leverage is a drag on the portfolio rate of return. This condition holds for the case in Part C, where the return on funds of 0.3 percent is less than the cost of borrowing of 0.3833 percent, and therefore, the portfolio return (0.1751 percent) is less than the return on funds.

    E. The bond dealer faces a credit risk even if he holds the collateral. The reason is that the value of the collateral may decline to such an extent that its market value falls below the amount lent. In such a situation, if the borrower defaults, the market value of the collateral will be insufficient to cover the amount lent.

CHAPTER 13

RELATIVE-VALUE METHODOLOGIES FOR GLOBAL CREDIT BOND PORTFOLIO MANAGEMENT

SOLUTIONS

Note: Many of the questions are conceptual in nature. The solutions offered are one interpretation, and there may be other valid views.

1. Relative value refers to ranking credit sectors, bond structures, issuers, and issues in terms of their expected performance over some future time period.
2. A. The dominant structure in the investment-grade credit market is the bullet structure with an intermediate maturity.
   B. There are three strategic portfolio implications of the bullet structure with an intermediate maturity:
      i. The dominance of bullet structures creates a scarcity value for structures with embedded call and put features, resulting in premium price for bonds with embedded call options. This "scarcity value" should be considered by managers in relative-value analysis of credit bonds.
      ii. Because long-dated maturities have declined as a percentage of outstanding credit debt, there is a lower effective duration of all outstanding credit debt and, as a result, a reduction in the aggregate sensitivity to interest-rate risk.
      iii. There will be increased use of credit derivatives, whether on a stand-alone basis or embedded in structured notes, so that investors and issuers can gain exposure to the structures they desire.
   C. High-yield issuers will continue to issue callable bond structures in order to have the opportunity to refinance at a lower credit spread should credit quality improve.
3. A. Yield curve placement is simply the positioning of a portfolio with respect to duration and yield curve risk. Trades involving yield curve placement are referred to as curve adjustment trades in the reading. Sector and quality allocations refer to allocations based

on relative value analysis of the different bond market sectors and quality sectors. Security selection involves the purchase or avoidance of individual issues based on some relative value basis.

B. For a manager who is evaluated relative to some bond index, the deviation of the portfolio from the benchmark in terms of yield curve exposure, sector exposure, quality exposure, and exposure to individual issues is the appropriate way to measure risk.

4. A. Scarcity value means that an issue will trade at a premium price due to a lack of supply (relative to demand) for that issue. This is the same as saying that the issue will trade at a narrower spread. If investors want exposure to a first-time issuer, the spread can be narrower than otherwise comparable issuers.

   B. Analytical models for valuing bonds with embedded put options assume the issuer will fulfill the obligation to repurchase an issue if the bondholder exercises the put option. For high-yield issuers, there is the credit risk associated with the potential inability to satisfy the put obligation. Thus for high-yield issuers, the credit risk may override the value for a putable issue derived from a valuation model.

5. In general, the top-down approach involves beginning with a macroeconomic outlook and making allocation decisions to sectors based on that outlook. With respect to credit in emerging markets, the top-down approach begins with the assessment of the economic outlook for emerging market countries and then basing the allocation of funds across emerging market credit issuers in different countries on that macroeconomic outlook. This is what Mr. Taylor means by "sovereign plus." The bottom-up approach focuses on the selection of corporate issuers in emerging market countries that are expected to outperform US credit issuers. This is what Mr. Taylor means by "US credits-plus."

6. A. Historical relations help a portfolio manager identify opportunities when current spreads are out of line and relative-value opportunities may be available. Liquidity considerations affect spreads and the ability to trade. Market segmentation means factors affecting supply and demand within sectors of the bond market due to impediments or restrictions on investors from reallocating funds across those bond sectors.

   B. Market segmentation may create relative value opportunities when spreads get out of line due to obstructions that prevent or impede investors from allocating funds to certain sectors due to regulatory constraints and asset/liability constraints. Market segmentation may affect the supply of bonds in a sector for the same reasons. In pursuit of the optimal timing to move into or out of a sector (industry category, maturity neighborhood, or structure) or individual issuer, historical analysis of spreads, based on mean-reversion analysis can help identify when spreads might revert to some "normal" equilibrium.

7. A. Spread curves show the relationship between spreads and maturity. They differ by issuer or sector in terms of the amount of the spread and the slope of the spread curve.

   B. Forward rates are derived from spot rates using arbitrage arguments. A forward spread, or an implied forward spread, can be derived in the same way. Also, forward rates were explained as basically hedgeable or breakeven rates—rates that will make an investor indifferent between two alternatives. For example, for default-free instruments a 2-year forward rate 3 years from now is a rate that will make an investor indifferent between investing in a 5-year zero-coupon default-free instrument or investing in a 3-year zero-coupon default-free instrument and reinvesting the proceeds for two more years after the 3-year instrument matures.

   A forward spread can be interpreted in the same way. For example, a 2-year forward spread 3 years from now is the credit spread that will make an investor indifferent to investing in a 5-year zero-coupon instrument of an issuer or investing in a 3-year zero-coupon instrument of the same issuer and reinvesting the proceeds from the maturing instrument in a 2-year zero-coupon instrument of the same issuer.

The forward spread is a breakeven spread because it is the spread that would make the investor indifferent between two alternative investments with different maturities over a given investment horizon.

C. Because a forward spread is one that will make an investor indifferent between two alternatives, a manager must compare his or her expectations relative to the forward spread. Relative-value analysis involves making this comparison between expected spread and what is built into market prices (i.e., forward spread).

8. Yield measures are poor indicators of total return realized by holding a security to maturity or over some investment horizon. Thus, an asset manager does not know what a yield pickup of, say, 20 basis points means for subsequent total return. A bond manager can pick up yield on a trade (holding credit quality constant), but on a relative value basis underperform an alternative issue with a lower yield over the manager's investment horizon.

   An example of this would be if at the beginning of the month, a portfolio manager sold the 5-year Ford issue at a spread of 140 basis points and purchased the 5-year General Motors issue at a spread of 150 basis points, for a yield pickup of 10 basis points. If the spread on the Ford issue continued to tighten throughout the month, while the General Motors issue's spread remained constant, the Ford issue would outperform the General Motors issue on a total return basis.

9. The reason suggested as to why heavy supply of new investment-grade credit issues will help spreads contract and enhance returns is that new primary bond valuations validate and enhance secondary valuations. In contrast, when new issuance declines sharply, secondary traders lose confirmation from the primary market and tend to require higher spreads.

10. A. The crossover sector refers to the sector with issuers whose ratings are between Ba2/BB and Baa3/BBB– by a major rating agency. These issuers are on the border between investment grade and high yield.

    B. A manager can purchase a below-investment grade issue that he believes will be upgraded to investment grade. If the manager is correct, then the issue will outperform due to spread narrowing resulting from the upgrade and also from increased liquidity as it becomes available to a broader class of investors.

11. A portfolio manager would consider implementing a credit-defense trade when the manager became increasingly concerned about geopolitical risk, the general economy, sector risk, or specific-issuer risk, which could lead to widening credit spreads.

12. The motivation is to increase portfolio liquidity.

13. A. The European credit market has been consistently homogeneous, having mostly high quality (rated Aa3/AA– and above) and intermediate maturity issues. So swap spreads were a good proxy for credit spreads. Because of the homogeneous character of the credit market in Europe, the swaps framework allows managers as well as issuers to more easily compare securities across fixed- and floating-rate markets. Moreover, in Europe, financial institutions such as commercial banks have been much more willing to use swap methodology to capture value discrepancies between the fixed- and floating-rate markets.

    B. US managers have embraced swap spreads for the MBS, CMBS, agency, and ABS sectors. This may gradually occur in the US credit markets as well to help facilitate relative value comparisons across non-US and non-credit sectors to US credit securities.

C. Individual investors understand the traditional nominal spread framework as a market convention. Moreover despite its limitations, this framework can be used across the entire credit-quality spectrum from Aaa's to B's. The disadvantage is that the nominal spread framework does not work very well for investors and issuers in comparing the relative attractiveness between the fixed- and floating-rate markets. This is the advantage of using the swap framework.

14. A. By buying ABC Corporation issue and entering into a 5-year swap to pay fixed and receive floating, the spread over Libor until the first reset date for the swap is:

Receive from ABC Corp. (6.00% + 120 bps)	7.20%
− Pay on swap (6.00% + 100 bps)	7.00%
+ Receive from swap	Libor
Net	Libor + 20 bps

Since Libor is 5.70%, the manager is locking in a rate of 5.90% (= 5.70% + 20 basis points) until the first reset date.

B. If the manager expects that interest rates will increase, total return performance will be better using the swap.

15. A. The manager is relying on primary market analysis. The manager believes that one of the reasons why the spread on single-A rated issues may be out of line in the fourth quarter of 1999 is due to the lack of single-A rated issues coming to market in that quarter. The manager expects that in the first quarter of 2000, there will be a surge of single-A rated issues that will come to market, resulting in a widening of spreads and thereby providing an opportunity to purchase single-A rated issues relatively cheaply versus BBB issues.

The assumption is that the attractive level of the corporate spread for single-A rated issuers is driven principally by new issuance and not any structural issue or other factor that determines corporate spreads. Furthermore, it is assumed that once the market is cleared of the increase in supply of single-A rated issuers, the spread will narrow and provide better performance relative to BBB rated issuers.

B. The keys to this strategy are 1) that the cash flows will in fact remain strong, 2) that the spread for these health care issuers are not justified by the strong cash flow despite concerns with healthcare reform, and 3) that investors in the bond market will recognize this (by some time period), resulting in a decline in the credit spread for these issuers.

16. The motivation for this strategy is that while investment-grade issues may decline due to stronger-than-anticipated economic growth, a good amount of spread reduction has already occurred in above BBB rated sectors. Thus, on a relative basis, the decline in corporate spreads on investment grade bonds due to stronger-than-anticipated growth will be primarily in BBB rated sectors. The assumption is that spreads will contract more in the BBB rated sector.

17. This relative value strategy has two elements to it. First, there appears to be an allocation to single-A rated corporates versus lower-quality corporates. Hence, it appears to be a credit-defense trade because of a concern with the economy slowing down. Moreover, there is an allocation within the single-A rated corporates to a sector—non-cyclical consumer non-durables—that is expected to outperform an alternative sector—cyclicals—should the economy slow down.

18. A. One can use mean-reversion analysis in this question as follows. For each issue, the number of standard deviations that the current spread is above the historical average (the mean spread for the past six months) is computed as:

Issue	Number of Standard Deviations Above Mean
A	(110 – 85)/25 = 1.0
B	(124 – 100)/10 = 2.4
C	(130 – 110)/15 = 1.3

Issue B has the largest deviation above the mean and is therefore the one more likely to contract. Actually, based on a normal distribution, the probability associated with realizing a specified number of standard deviation above the mean can be determined.

B. The assumptions are that 1) the spreads will revert back to their historic means and 2) there have been no structural changes in the market that would render the historical mean and standard deviation useless for the analysis.

19. Ms. Xu should first explain that callable bonds exhibit negative convexity when interest rates decline, while noncallable bonds exhibit positive convexity. This means that when rates decline, the price appreciation for a callable bond will not be as great as an otherwise noncallable bond. Since the management team expects a significant drop in interest rates in the next quarter, to better participate in the rise in bond prices, there was a shift to noncallable credit securities.

    All mortgage pass-through securities exhibit negative convexity. However, low-coupon issues exhibit less negative convexity than high-coupon issues. That is, there will be greater price appreciation for low-coupon issues when rates decline. Given the anticipated decline in interest rates, the low-coupon issues will appreciate more and hence the reason for the shift to such issues.

20. Ms. Smith could sell retail issues and use the proceeds to purchase US dollar-denominated corporate bonds of European issuers. This would be consistent with her expectation of underperformance of the retail sector and outperformance of the European corporate sector. She could make her purchases in the new issue market, if she believes new issues will be attractively priced.

    Ms. Smith should use credit analysis to select which issues to buy or sell within each sector. She must consider the possibility of a risk premium in the European corporate sector, as some managers cannot purchase bonds in that sector. Seasonality may also be a factor, depending on the timing of her purchases/sales.

21. C is correct. The Yield Curve Plus Fund is using key rate duration to enhance portfolio returns. Key rate duration attempts to profit from non-parallel shifts in the yield curve.
22. C is correct. Contingent immunization is a mix of the passive and active styles. Therefore, it is closest to the Yield Curve Plus Fund.
23. A is correct. Both statements regarding contingent immunization are correct.
24. B is correct. The Long-Term US Corporate Bond Index's duration is closest to that of Hanover-Green's liabilities and reflects the corporate bonds that form the bulk of their assets.
25. A is correct. Warren is most likely correct regarding the effect on spreads and the probability of the bonds being callable. During most years, increases in issuance are associated with market-spread contraction. Bullet structures without call, put, or sinking fund options have come to dominate the credit market.
26. A is correct. OAS has limited use in the analysis of speculative grade bonds because default risk is excluded from the calculation.

ABOUT THE CFA PROGRAM

The Chartered Financial Analyst® designation (CFA®) is a globally recognized standard of excellence for measuring the competence and integrity of investment professionals. To earn the CFA charter, candidates must successfully pass through the CFA Program, a global graduate-level self-study program that combines a broad curriculum with professional conduct requirements as preparation for a wide range of investment specialties.

Anchored by a practice-based curriculum, the CFA Program is focused on the knowledge identified by professionals as essential to the investment decision-making process. This body of knowledge maintains current relevance through a regular, extensive survey of practicing CFA charterholders across the globe. The curriculum covers 10 general topic areas, ranging from equity and fixed-income analysis to portfolio management to corporate finance, all with a heavy emphasis on the application of ethics in professional practice. Known for its rigor and breadth, the CFA Program curriculum highlights principles common to every market so that professionals who earn the CFA designation have a thoroughly global investment perspective and a profound understanding of the global marketplace.

www.cfainstitute.org

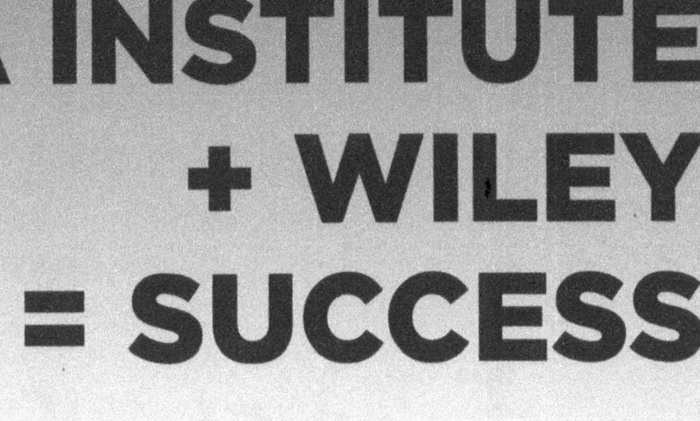

978-1-118-99949-3
Hardcover
$100.00 US
$110.00 CAN
£70.00 UK

978-1-118-99950-9
Paper
$45.00 US
$50.00 CAN
£30.99 UK

John Wiley & Sons and CFA Institute are proud to present the *CFA Institute Investment Series* geared specifically for industry professionals and graduate-level students. This cutting-edge series focuses on the most important topics in the finance industry. The authors of these books are themselves leading industry professionals and academics who bring their wealth of knowledge and expertise to you.

The series provides clear, practitioner-driven coverage of the knowledge and skills critical to investment analysts, portfolio managers, and financial advisors.

978-1-118-10537-5
$100.00 US
$120.00 CAN/£70.00 UK

978-0-470-91580-6
$95.00 US
$114.00 CAN/£65.00 UK

978-0-470-62400-5
$100.00 US
$120.00 CAN/£70.00 UK

978-0-470-57143-9
$100.00 US
$120.00 CAN/£70.00 UK

978-0-470-05220-4
$100.00 US
$119.99 CAN/£70.00 UK

978-1-118-99947-9
$100.00 US
$110.00 CAN/£70.00 UK

978-0-470-08014-6
$100.00 US
$119.99 CAN/£70.00 UK

978-1-118-10536-8
$100.00 US
$120.00 CAN/£70.00 UK

Get these titles and companion Workbooks at wiley.com or cfainstitute.org
Available in print and e-book format.

Wiley is a registered trademark of John Wiley & Sons, Inc.
CFA Institute logo is a registered trademark of CFA Institute.

WILEY

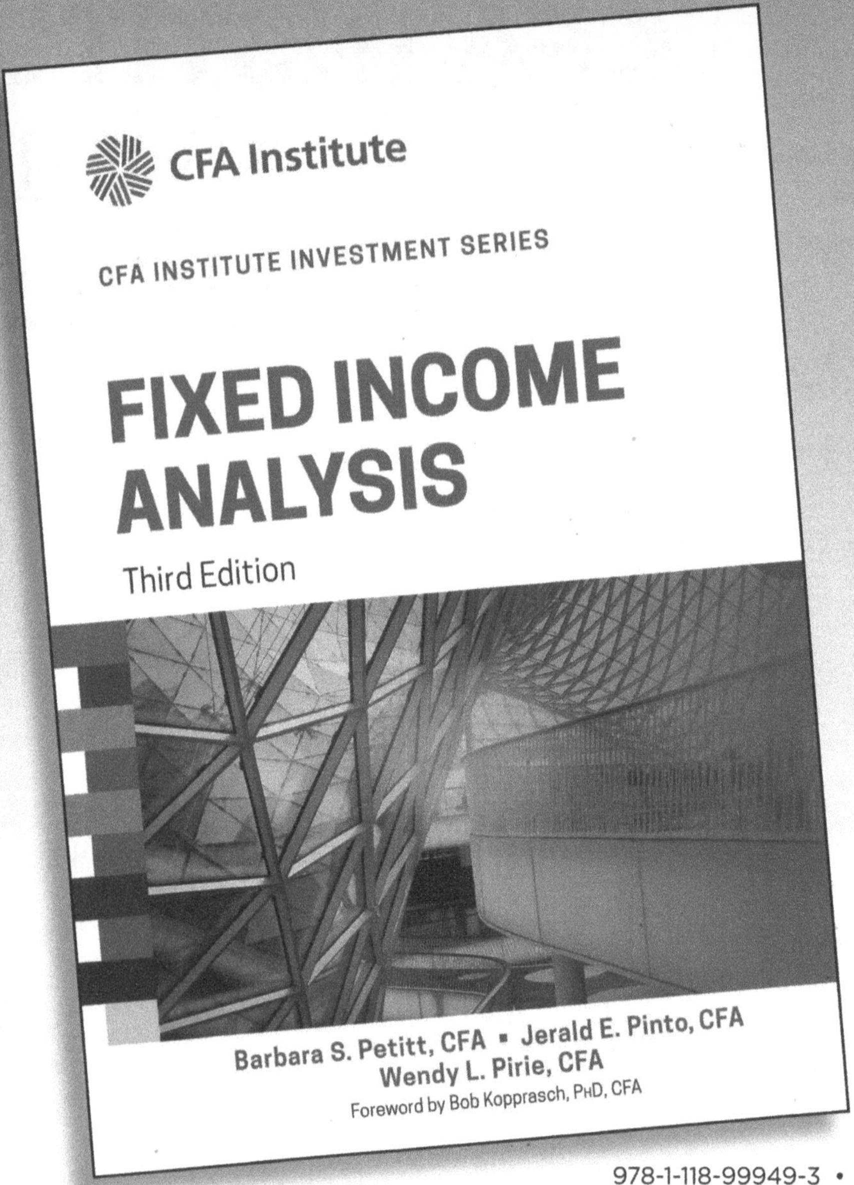

CFA Institute

CFA INSTITUTE INVESTMENT SERIES

FIXED INCOME ANALYSIS

Third Edition

Barbara S. Petitt, CFA ▪ Jerald E. Pinto, CFA
Wendy L. Pirie, CFA
Foreword by Bob Kopprasch, PhD, CFA

978-1-118-99949-3 • Hardcover
$100.00 US/$110.00 CAN/£70.00 UK

The **definitive guide** to
fixed-income portfolio management,
revised and updated.

Available at wiley.com, cfainstitute.org, and wherever books are sold.

Wiley is a registered trademark of John Wiley & Sons, Inc.
CFA Institute logo is a registered trademark of CFA Institute.